Robert Lewis
and his son Jake

Life-and-death struggles of the
Wigan and North Wales mining
communities in the 19th century

Mold High Street (from the Cross) by Pring & Price, Mold

Robert Lewis
and his son Jake

Life-and-death struggles of the
Wigan and North Wales mining
communities in the 19th century

by

Richard D. Lewis

Robert Lewis and his son Jake
Life-and-death struggles of the Wigan and North Wales mining communities in the 19th century

First published in hardback in 2013 by Transcreen Publications, Warnford.

Transcreen Publications
The Old Stables
Warnford
Hampshire
SO32 3LH
United Kingdom

Tel. +44 (0)1962 77 11 11
Fax +44 (0)1962 77 10 50
Email info@transcreen.net

ISBN: 978-0-9534398-5-0

Layout and cover design by David Lewis.
Photographs and cover painting by the author.

Printed and bound in Great Britain by TJ International Ltd, Padstow, Cornwall

MIX
Paper from
responsible sources
FSC® C013056

for my twin grandsons, Robert and Jake Lewis

Robert   Jake

CONTENTS

Other books by Richard D. Lewis

The Road from Wigan Pier
The Billingers
English You Need
Vous-souvenez-vous?
Reading for Adults
Humour across Frontiers
Finland Cultural Lone Wolf
Cross-Cultural Communication – A Visual Approach
When Cultures Collide
When Teams Collide
The Cultural Imperative

About the Author

Born in the depressed 1930s into a family of Lancashire miners, a piece of coal's throw from Wigan Pier, Richard Lewis grew up in the rough-hewn homeland of Rugby League, with its awesomely deep collieries, its massive, gaunt cotton mills, black-faced pitmen and raw-boned pit lassies. Though loving his bleak environment, Lewis resolved to better his circumstances by exploiting his inborn, unique ability to master foreign languages at a rapid pace. He spoke three at the age of 12, staggered through university on a shoe-string and emerged with degrees in Spanish, Italian and French. By the time he was 25, he spoke 10 languages as well as the Wigan miners' dialect.

Descendant of five generations of Welsh and Lancashire miners, he tried his hand at various jobs and pursuits in a variety of countries. He was successively a railway carriage cleaner, a farm labourer, journalist, teacher, school director, university lecturer, interpreter, BBC scriptwriter, news broadcaster, film actor, yachtsman, speech writer and author (won the U.S. Book of the Month Club selection in 1997). For three years he was personal tutor to Empress Michiko of Japan and is currently cross-cultural adviser to the World Bank. He was knighted by the President of Finland in 1997 and promoted to the rank of Knight Commander in 2009.

Acknowledgements

In piecing together the two-part career of Robert Lewis, my great-grandfather, I was greatly and unhesitatingly aided by the following individuals and institutions, to whom I am extremely grateful:

Curator Peter Francis of the Gladstone Library
Davies, Alan, author of Coal Mining in Lancashire and Cheshire
W. Kelly, NUM Lancs.
The Librarians at Mold Library, N. Wales
Hawarden Archives Office
Alex Miller and Joan Livesey of Wigan Archives Service
Frank Smith of the Labour Party
The Registrar Office, Llwynegrin Hall, Mold
Robert Bradley
Bob & Jocelyn Coburn
Judith Johnson of Mold Parish Church
Pat Champness
Wigan Leisure & Culture Trust
Chief Executive, Mold Town Hall, Fred Boneham
David Lewis
Wigan Heritage Centre

While this book is dedicated to my twin grandsons – Robert and Jake Lewis – I would not wish to omit from this volume the names of a number of miners whom I have known and been close to. Many are, of course, blood relations. Most of them spent their whole working lives underground.

Robert Lewis
Jake Lewis
John Lewis
Jim Parr
Hugh Parr
Jim Birchall
Jack Birchall
Harry Wagstaff
Ronnie James
Ben Lowe
Tom Lowe
Jack Lowe
Billy Lowe
Lloyd Lowe
Joe Gormley
Bob Wyke
George Buxton
Charlie Buxton

Foreword

Robert Lewis – my great-grandfather – was born on 19 February 1832 in Mold, North Wales, worked down the pit from the age of 9 till he died at the age of 48, became a natural miners' leader in his early twenties and emerged in the 1870s as one of the greatest miners' orators of his era. In 1869-70 he was one of the co-founders of the AAM (Amalgamated Association of Miners) which can be regarded as the first trade union in the world. Successive miners' leaders such as John L. Lewis (USA) and Joe Gormley owed much to Robert Lewis' fiery oratory and human reputation which gave miners considerable influence in the 20th century until Margaret Thatcher broke Arthur Scargill's flawed leadership in 1985.

Robert Lewis, a fully-fledged Welshman, fluent in both Welsh and English, had two careers as a miners' leader and orator – one in North Wales and one in the heart of the South Lancashire mining community in Wigan. When his grandson Richard Lewis – my father – died as the last of his generation in 1977, I received a visit from two officials of the British Labour Party, who asked me if I could supply them with details of the Welsh half of my great-grandfather's career, in Mold during the years 1832-1856. This I was unable to do, as I knew only of his activities in the Wigan coalfield. The two Labour men stressed the importance of Robert Lewis to the early development of the Federation of Miners' Associations and went on to do further research on their own, with some, but limited success.

I for my own part had resolved at that time to write his biography but was prevented from doing so by the development of my own career and, more importantly, by lack of information about his early activities in Wales.

In 2009-10, I was able to benefit from 'semi-retirement' to make several trips to Mold and other parts of Flintshire to hunt down records of Robert Lewis in various archives and newspaper cuttings of the period from the 1830s until the Mold Riot of 1869. I was reasonably, though not completely, successful in digging out information of the period and environment, but almost despaired of achieving satisfaction until, one day, I had a wonderful breakthrough.

Daniel Owen is regarded by many as one of the greatest Welsh novelists. Born in Mold, he based his novels on local subjects, especially the mining community. The chief librarian in Mold library told me that Owen had written a blockbuster of a novel in Welsh, entitled "Rhys Lewis". He considered it was closely related to the mining activities in mid-19th century Mold in which my great-grandfather had featured. There was only one problem – the novel had been printed in its thousands in Welsh, but the small edition in English had long been out of print. I cannot read Welsh, so I asked where I might get my hands on the English translation.

"There is only one known copy left in the world," he replied, "and of course it is carefully guarded."

"Where is it?" I asked.

"Over there on the top shelf."

"May I read it?" I asked.

"Yes, but only in the library," he replied. "It cannot be removed."

"May I photo-copy it?" I pleaded.

"Yes, but only 10 pages at a time. Copyright, you know…"

"How many pages has the book?"

Statue of Daniel Owen, Mold (photograph by Ray Bibby)

"Four hundred and thirty-two."

"So I'll have to come in on 43 separate days?"

"I'm afraid so."

However, I soon received a lesson about Welsh skill in negotiation and discretion. While the chief librarian was out for lunch, his kindly and sympathetic assistant let me race down to an ancient photocopy machine and copy the entire book – page by page – in a frantic hour and a half. (Modern Welshmen take long lunches). I paid my £15 and scampered out of the building with my precious document and spent the next two days devouring it.

What I read – and the information it provided – exceeded all my expectations. Not only does this remarkable, moving novel relate in detail the social and religious life of the mining community of North Wales over 150 years ago, but the poignant hero of the book – a young mining face-worker and orator – is unmistakably my great-grandfather. The story that unfolds depicts a fiery young man who, in his early twenties, spoke so eloquently on behalf of the suppressed miners that his popularity inspired his generation to rise up against the blatant injustices they had suffered so long. The author Daniel Owen identifies his hero so closely with my great-grandfather that he actually calls him Robert Lewis in the novel, where his influential mother – Mary Lewis – has the same name as Robert Lewis' wife in real life.

The richness of the story derives mainly from the long, passionate dialogues between Robert and the puritanical Mary who, though approving his crusade on the pitmen's behalf, is deeply concerned over his weakening affinity with the chapel and his frequent departure from maxims laid out in the scriptures, to which she so vehemently adheres. These intensely probing conversations between mother and son have helped me greatly in getting inside the mind and attitudes of my worthy forebear and giving me insights into the conflicting mentalities of his co-workers and figures of authority who together wrote the history of 19th century mining in North Wales.

The novel is faithful in its adherence to Robert Lewis's early life and efforts, but differs in one essential matter – the manner of his death. In the book he is killed in a pit explosion – the fate of many miners of the period – whereas the real-life Robert Lewis, avoiding such a tragic end, emigrated to Wigan in Lancashire, with wife Mary and his young son, John Lewis. There the second major chapter of his life unfolds, about which I have sufficient documentation and knowledge of the area, in which I was born.

The second half of Daniel Owen's book deals with the somewhat tortured life of Rhys Lewis, Robert's younger brother, who emerges as a kind of anti-hero and for years wrestles with his conscience and aspirations to godliness, becoming eventually "Minister of Bethel." The author describes his work as an autobiography, and there is little doubt it is such, as Owen was known for his aberrations from scriptural edicts – drinking, womanising and other "depravities" which he frequently refers to but does not detail. This part of the novel is of less interest to me as it hardly deals with the miners and lacks the excitement arising from their struggles. It does, however, give me a fuller picture of the religious life of 19th century Flintshire – an atmosphere that certainly influenced Robert Lewis in his early upbringing. Furthermore, in the 1920s and 30s another Robert Lewis – one of his grandsons – achieved no little fame as a Methodist preacher in the chapels of the South Lancs. coalfield, before eventually becoming Mayor of Wigan in 1930.

Chapter 1

Mold in History

The area around Mold has had settlements from the earliest times, and the most important archeological discovery from the earliest periods of settlement has to be the "Gold Cape" which is housed in the British Museum in London. This beautifully decorated cape was discovered near the Chester Road in 1831 on the "Hill of Elves". Dating from the Bronze Age, there has been a movement of late to try and bring this priceless example of craftsmanship back to Mold. The cape weighs 560 grams and was produced from a single gold ingot. This golden relic provided inspiration in the naming of the town's "Wetherspoons" pub.

The Normans established Mold as a fixed settlement. The place name Mold originates from the Norman French *mont-hault* (high hill) and is recorded as Mohald in a document of 1254. The Welsh language place name of Yr Wyddgrug is recorded as Gythe Cruc in a document of 1280-81 and comes from the words *Yr* (the), *gwydd* (tomb, sepulchre) and *crug* (mound). The Normans built the Motte and Bailey Castle on the strategic Bailey Hill during the reign of William Rufus and you can still view the outlines of the Norman hill site. Mold, being a frontier town, changed hands between the Normans and the Welsh a number of times from 1140 to 1270 (the most notable Welsh occupation being from 1199 to 1240 after the conquest by Llewelyn the Great). Edward I finally resolved the status of Mold and all of Wales in the conquest ending 1277. At this time the Lordship of Mold was held by the Montalts but by 1329 the Lordship had settled on the Stanleys.

It was the Stanleys who instigated the construction of the Parish Church of Mold to mark the victory of Henry Tudor in the Battle of Bosworth in 1485 (Lord Stanley's wife was the mother of Henry Tudor). During a stroll around this church it is well worth inspecting the detailed ornamentation – you can spot all the emblems of the Stanleys – the eagle and claw, the three legs of man and the pelican. The Stanleys declared for the King during the Civil War (1642-49) and contributed a force of 1,000.

The extensive development of mining in the area during the 18th and 19th centuries defined Mold as an industrial town. The Ironmaster John "Iron Mad" Wilkinson leased the Llyn-y-Pandy lead mine near Gwernaffield and introduced large scale production methods including a smelting works. By 1835, there were offices of nine lead companies in the town and the town had expanded rapidly. The globalisation of lead mining, in particular the development of the vast mines in the USA, was the downfall of the small local mines and almost all had closed by the end of the First World War. However, the most important mining product was coal. The area had a wealth of cannel coal located in thick seams. During the 19th century there were up to eight working collieries in the town. Mold had its share of mining disasters – in 1837 the Argoed colliery was flooded and 31 miners were killed, including the novelist Daniel Owen's father and brothers. Coal mining declined at the start of the 20th century with the last colliery, Bromfield Colliery, closing during the First World War. The town also experienced periods of social unrest in the form of strikes and riots due to disagreements about pay and working conditions. One such conflagration resulted in tragedy and is known as the Mold Riot of 1869, which is described in detail in Chapter 13.

St. Mary's Church, Mold. Original watercolour by Gwyn Harvey

The Mold area is also famous for creating an old saying – that of being at loggerheads – which means being in disagreement. A previous landlord of the 'We Three Loggerheads' public house has recounted the story behind this as follows:

During the 1780s a local landowner and a vicar from the parish of Llanferres were in constant disagreement regarding some issue and to try and resolve the problem, the landlord of the Loggerheads Inn decided to call a meeting between the two at the inn. Although not clear whether the matter was entirely resolved at this meeting, one of the parties, Richard Wilson, decided to paint the sign for the Loggerheads with the writing "We Three Loggerheads". The thinking behind this was there were two people at the Loggerheads in disagreement plus the third person, whoever it may be in the future, looking at the sign. Hence, locally, and later nationally, the phrase caught on that to be "at Loggerheads" was to be in disagreement, whereas all it initially meant was being at the Loggerheads public house! The sign and the inn are still there today at the entrance to the Loggerheads Country Park.

With its industries long gone, modern Mold enjoys a less violent reputation as a "cittaslow" – a slow food town. Indeed it was the first town in Wales to achieve this distinction. It has a market every Wednesday and Saturday, at which much fresh produce can be obtained. For speciality and fresh local food, the Celyn Farmers' Market is held on the first Saturday of every month in Mold and on the third Sunday of the month in nearby Northop. The Mold Food and Drink Festival is held during September each year. The festival, which has become very famous, has a central event area on the edge of the town centre.

Mold has a museum, a recognised arts centre (Clwyd Theatre Cymru) and hosted the National Eistedfodd in 1923, 1991 and 2007. Mold's two secondary schools serve the town and surrounding villages. With approximately 1800 pupils, the Alun School is the largest school in the county. It is adjoined by the only Welsh language secondary school in Flintshire, Ysgol Maes Garmon. According to the 2001 UK Census, Mold had a population of 9,568.

Modern Mold, with its clean, cosy streets, flourishing markets, 15th century parish church and air of bustling prosperity, is in marked contrast to the socially stricken community that Robert Lewis grew up in. Workers and owners (masters) were in perpetual and bitter conflict from the end of the 18th century and throughout the 19th. The town was blighted by the harsh environmental conditions caused by an industrial revolution in its infancy. Britain, as the site of the world's first industrial revolution, had all the teething problems of such a development which other countries, industrialising later, were able to avoid. Wales and Lancashire, on account of their mineral wealth (principally coal) took the brunt of the revolution's assault on human quality of life and health in working conditions as bad, or probably worse, than those described by Dickens in London.

The next chapter deals with such conditions as they were in mid-19th century Mold and North Wales.

Old map of central Mold

Chapter 2

From Schoolboy to Orator

Such was the infant mortality rate in most of Chinese history, it was a Chinese tradition for couples to have many children in the hope that one or two of them might survive to take care of them in their old age. A similar situation existed among the working classes in North Wales throughout most of the 19th century. When Jacob Lewis (coal miner, born 1803) of Llwynegrin married Elizabeth Evans of Llanfair in 1825 they went on to found a family of eight children, only one of whom was able to contribute to their support. This was their third son Robert, whose life story is related in this book. It is an interesting story, inasmuch as Robert Lewis, who survived to become one of the most significant miners' leaders of the 19th century, was born into poverty and tragedy typical of the communities around Mold at that time.

Jacob's and Elizabeth's first son, Edward (born 1826) died at the age of two. Their second son, Thomas (born 1829), named after his grandfather (born 1762), was still alive when Robert entered the world in February 1832, but died five months later, aged three. Great would have been the delight of the parents with the birth of Lewis twins, Edward and Bridget, on 24 August 1834. Bridget, however, lived only three weeks. Robert had barely got to know his younger brother Edward when he, too, succumbed at the age of two (just as the first Edward had done).

The first sibling whom Robert got to know and protect, was his sister Elizabeth, born in 1838 when he was six. We say protect, for Robert was sent to work down the mine at the age of 9 and his miserable boy miner's wage would nevertheless find its way into his mother's apron to help buy food for the small family, including two baby brothers, Edward (again!) and John, born 1840 and 1843.

Father Jacob himself was ailing, his strength attenuated by exhausting daily underground toil and, like many of his co-workers, succumbed to heart failure at the age of 45. This meant that Robert, 16 at the time of his father's death, was the only breadwinner for the family of five. And bread it usually was, for the staple fare for miners' families at that time was 'browes' – pieces of bread soaked in hot water with a little dripping or butter added – meat and potatoes were only available on pay-days if Robert had filled enough tubs. Fortunately Robert, in spite of this meagre diet, had grown to be a strapping young man and by the age of 18 had the reputation of being one of the best face-workers in the group of colliers in the Mold area. The arduous nature of the toil and hazards on the coal-face in the old-fashioned and perilous pits of North Wales and Lancashire are described in detail in a later chapter of this book by one of Robert's sons (also a coalminer from the age of 9). Suffice it to say at this point that Robert – a remarkable individual by any measure – not only provided the wherewithal for his humble dependents during the next decade, but hastened to procure books for his self-education and enlightenment in the time available to him after his 8-10 hour shifts. An avid reader, he read in English and Welsh, thus acquiring bi-lingual fluency which was to stand him in good stead when he began to address miners not only in Wales but over the border.

*   *   *

But let us go back to Robert's modest beginnings. He was born, in the words of Daniel Owen, "in the light of a halfpenny candle between

Bethesda Chapel, New Street, Mold

2 and 3 a.m." Most miners' children were born at home in conditions lacking the basic sanitary requirements and medical attention
that today assure the newborn of a good chance of an unblemished
birth and healthy infancy. In the 19th century mining community
of Mold, more infants died than lived. To his parents' relief, Robert
survived and his first memories were of carrying his baby brother
down the dark staircase of the unpretentious one-up-and-one-down
terraced miners' cottage of Garden Place. The Lewis dwelling was one
of a row of ten red-brick houses, long since demolished.

The front doors opened directly on the 'street' – an unsealed piece
of stony grey earth which served as a playground for the two dozen
or so surviving infants of the ten families housed in the row. As most
boys were sent down the mine at the age of nine or ten, the age group
was two to eight. During school hours children from five to eight
received their all-too-brief education. The remaining infants, watched

over by two or three mothers, spent the mornings and most of the afternoons outside, winter and summer, shouting, screaming, quarrelling and often fighting over pieces of bread or biscuits or the odd carrot or cheap toy. The children, offspring of three or four generations of miners' stock, were almost uniformly undersized for their age, pale and sharp-eyed and lacking the cherubic features and rosy complexions of children from the agricultural countryside, who often made their appearance with their farmer parents on market days. Fragile, however, they were not; their outdoor exposure, constant scrambling and wrestling, mean competition for tid-bits or privileges, all served to harden their small bodies and sharpen their young minds. Though relatively under-nourished, they displayed the self-replenishing energy of children everywhere and if the facilities for their fun and play were limited, their infantile zest and ambitions were not.

Robert partook of this daily melée from the age of two and gambolled with the rest of them. More than half were girls; among the boys, especially the five-year-olds, there was keen competition for leadership. Who would be 'cock of the yard'? Size and physical strength often decided these matters and bullying was not uncommon. Robert, neither bigger nor smaller than the average, developed an early sturdiness both of body and spirit and defended himself adequately in the frequent brawls. What was noticeable about him was that though he won most of his fights, he rarely showed undue aggression. At an early age he displayed a tendency to defend weaker children and resisted bullies stoutly. In due course he became *de facto* cock of the yard but did not lay claim to the title, letting another boy call himself 'cock'. It was noticeable, however, that the nominal cock kept well away from Robert when things heated up. My grandfather – a tough old character himself in the 1930s – always mentioned this characteristic of Robert's – his insistence on justice, but by non-violent means.

Another trait which emerged in his teens was his facility for wit and self-expression. Though slow with his fists, he was ready with his tongue (too ready, said people in authority). My grandfather inherited the same wit and humour, though he had no oratorical aspirations. By the time Elizabeth Lewis and the two younger siblings, Edward and John, entered the street fray, Robert was unable to shelter them, as he had gone first to school and then down the pit. We have no details of their early days. Now, however we must follow Robert to school.

*   *   *

At the time of his birth there were only two schools in Mold, one run by a scholarly gentleman with the name of Smith. It was seen as a superior type of institution and the tall, thin, grey-headed Smith, dressed conservatively in black, his bespectacled face always exuding intellectuality, was regarded in some awe by the townspeople on account of his reputation for speaking several languages and actually seeing to it that his students learnt something. Only the gentry and well-to-do were able to send their children to Mr Smith's school – quite beyond the pecuniary reach of the miners' families. Not that the strictly Calvinist Methodist Elizabeth Lewis would have sent Robert to his school in any event, since he was C. of E., not Chapel, and moreover, grew a moustache. She used to see him taking his Sunday afternoon stroll, when he should have been at home "pondering the Word and the Doctrine" and she had heard that he read irreligious books in his spare time, in English to boot, which did nothing to allay her mistrust of him. Yes, his students acquired knowledge, but Elizabeth basically did not believe in education *per se*. She often said that no good came of over-education and that "too much of that sort of thing had led many a man to the gallows." She considered that the children of the poor, who could not afford much schooling anyway, would do well enough if they read and memorized sufficient chapters of the Scriptures, which would guide them through life, and on the Right Path at that.

In consequence of her views, Robert, destined to go down the mine at the age of 9, was sent for four brief years to the 'other school' in Mold – a slovenly-organized institution run by an ex-soldier, who cared not a jot for learning, but only for the penny a week he extracted from the miners' families to pay for their attendance. For their money the boys received more canings than lessons and the depredations of this institution are described vividly by Daniel Owen who, four years younger than Robert Lewis, bore witness to the futility of the set-up and the greed and blatant cruelty of the hypocritical head master.

Robert related to my grandfather that he learnt nothing from his teacher. But he developed such a hatred of school and school-rooms that, at a very early age, he took it upon himself to procure books, usually in English, to begin to explore the wonderful worlds of geography, history, the richness of the English language itself and subsequently the political undertones which permeated these subjects and indeed his own environment and position.

*   *   *

Parallel to his school education – miserable though it was – Robert received religious instruction. Chapel members belonged to the Society, an affiliate of which was the Children's Society, or, as it was often called, the Children's Meeting. Six or seven children usually attended once a week throughout the year, winter and summer. Attendance was compulsory, inasmuch as if you were an absentee it would earn a reprimand; chronic absenteeism would result in punish-ment of some kind.

Robert's mother Elizabeth was known as a 'Methodist of the Methodists' – that is to say, she was a strict observer of the edicts of the Scriptures, particularly with regard to the observance of the Sabbath. Robert, as a good son and a fine example of youthful con-scientiousness, obeyed his mother's wishes and hardly ever missed a Children's Meeting. Mary would send him every week with a 'new verse' to recite and it seems that he was both diligent and competent in performing this duty. He was, however, of an independent mind, and, though dutiful, began to question certain aspects of the Society. In later life he was well-known for his quick perception and ability to seize the point. Chapel services were long and often gloomy. As a boy he was frequently bored and began to lose patience with the more pedantic preachers. It is said he once advanced the long finger of the chapel clock when the preacher was briefly indisposed. Without being an absolute trickster, he developed a tendency to poke fun at anything he considered banal or pompous. As an older boy of 15, he taught a Sunday class to half a dozen boys aged five to seven. They were of course fond of well-known children's stories and Robert used them as a vehicle for defining good and evil. He had already been working down the mine for six years and he gave the stories a little twist of his own, so that the Three Bears sat in the front pew of the Chapel and the Seven Dwarfs worked down his own pit and had names like Tubby and Cannel and Cage-winder, while Red Riding Hood's grandmother and the Big Bad Wolf sang duets together.

His sense of humour notwithstanding, Robert year by year seems to have grown more restless with the exigencies and atmosphere of the Children's Society and the Chapel itself. In Mold at that time, as in other parts of Wales, there existed ongoing friction between Church and Chapel. A similar situation existed in nearby Lancashire, though there it was more triangular, as there were a greater number of Roman Catholics. Welsh miners were largely Chapel and felt that church folk looked down on them. This led them to discipline themselves more earnestly and many, like Elizabeth Lewis, became fervently devout. Robert noticed that the Methodist Society gathered weekly to castigate themselves mentally and proclaim how bad they were. He could not stomach this pious behaviour, particularly when he saw that Church people, hypocritical as he thought they were, did not indulge in this form of self-flagellation. Daniel Owen commented that "Church people thought they were good, when they really were bad, while Chapel people thought they were bad, though really they were good."

Robert did not think they were all that good, though he did not find them guilty of the sins they attributed to themselves. They saw themselves lacking in godliness, discipline, observance of doctrine, adequate piety. He worried more about their narrow-mindedness and hypocrisy, lack of tolerance, holier-than-thou postures and lack of invention or originality. Though he never missed chapel, he hated

Sundays, as the enforced idleness of the Sabbath got on his nerves. After toiling five or six days a week on the coal face, he craved either recreation or some creative activity at the week-end. This was denied to him by his fellow chapel-goers and his mother, who, when he was young, would not even let him look at a toy on Sundays, let alone play with children she disapproved of. Robert never lost his unbounded love for his mother and he never sought solace in drink, as many other pitmen did, but his views on what constituted good and evil diverged from those of his mother as time went by. As far as the members of the Society were concerned, he gradually distanced himself from their aspirations to saintliness, though he never attacked them directly. His reputation for wit and irony grew as he got older and he fell out of favour to some extent among those members who were aware of his silent criticism.

Robert's unease with his fellow chapellers' sanctimoniousness was a minor issue compared with his growing disquiet and unfolding resentment with regard to the wretched plight and miserable working conditions and remuneration of the Welsh coal miners.

*   *   *

In his quest for self-education and further enlightenment, Robert Lewis read everything he could get his hands on – mostly in English. From an early age he sensed that his fellow miners, with whom he toiled shoulder to shoulder, month in and month out, had little hope of bettering their lot on account of their profound ignorance of the world outside the pit, pub and chapel. Working hours were cruelly long, leisure pitifully short, exhaustion ingrained. How could these men in a vicious circle of gruelling work, fitful sleep and perennial under-nourishment, ever widen their horizons and aspirations – especially when spending half their waking hours one thousand feet below ground?!

What was remarkable about Robert Lewis was that in his early teens, although working a full shift and undergoing all the hardships referred to above, he had the clarity of mind to seek a way out of this brutal predicament and equip himself mentally to lead his fellow miners (and many others) out of it, even though it took more than three decades of strife, including a massacre in his home town (the Riot of Mold) that was to bring about a conclusive shift in British crowd control involving the police and military forces.

Research into Robert Lewis's early career raises more questions than it provides answers. A revolt against the despicable conditions of Welsh and Lancashire miners in the 19th century was ultimately inevitable, given the political developments and assertion of human rights in the aftermath of the Industrial Revolution. In the British Isles and throughout the continent of Europe, injustices were addressed, vested interests were defended, victories and setbacks succeeded each other, society became polarized. Robert Lewis, both in his youth and middle age, emerged as a central figure in these struggles not only in Flintshire, but in the far more prolific coal-producing area around Wigan and St Helens. Why did it fall upon **him** to assume the role of working men's champion? What spark ignited his unfailing energy, inspiring oratory, his unswerving pursuit of justice? Where did it all come from?

If one looks at the particulars of his humble birth and depressing personal environment, one would have to conclude that he was an unlikely candidate to succeed in confrontations with the unforgiving forces of England's Victorian Establishment. To begin with, he was lucky to survive at all, as the two brothers born before him died at the ages of two and three and the twins appearing not long after his birth passed away with equal rapidity. He was born in poverty and tragedy, barely having access to sufficient nourishment to rebound from these setbacks. Everything seemed against him – his road to strength, his chances of schooling, his choice of work, his hopes of social mobility, his very survival as a consequential, productive human being. His ailing father gave him little guidance and died when Robert was 16. His mother, though loving enough, disapproved of education in general and he was sent down the mine at the age of nine to alleviate the family's poverty-stricken situation. There was no

hope of benevolence of any kind from his employers, as the owners
of Leeswood Colliery were notorious for their rapacity and exploitation of the hapless miners. His chapel membership afforded him the
comfort of belonging to a group – the link between the chapel and the
mining community was strong – but worthy souls as they were, their
socio-political influence was minimal in mid-century and Robert's
own poor opinion of the uprightness of some of the established pillars
of the congregation resulted in his seeking support from the chapel
on only rare occasions such as their providing facilities for meetings.

In short, Robert Lewis, penniless and often hungry, lacking
formal education, uneasy with the local concept of religion, weak-
ened by exhausting and unhealthy work under ground, lacking any
connections or even strong familial support, started with all the
disadvantages and none of the advantages of an aspiring political
reformer. It is possible that the apparent hopelessness of his quest contributed towards his resilience and drive. All who knew him perceived
his crusading nature and his open tendency to self-sacrifice. He was
essentially reformist, not out of any desire to enter politics but explic-
itly to find an escape route from the grinding daily misery of his work
mates, their families and his own mother and siblings. In the event,
he devoted his whole life to their cause. They say that politics is the
last refuge of a scoundrel; this adage could not apply to a man who,
though an accepted leader, invariably worked a full shift on most of
the days when he attended or conducted meetings. Both the Welsh
and Lancashire miners were well aware of this, and it is perhaps the
main reason why he commanded their allegiance.

Admired he certainly was. By the time he was 20, his fame as a
speaker and miners' leader was spreading rapidly across the whole of
Flintshire. Daniel Owen, his younger neighbour and novelist-to-be,
also from a poor mining family, went personally to his meetings and
described him in these words:

"On leaving chapel, Will took me by the arm and said 'Let's go to
the Colliers' Meeting'. I was unaware of the event, but my friend knew
of every public gathering that took place. It was an open air meeting,

the night was a lovely one in summer. On approaching, I heard a great noise, and shouts of 'Hear, hear' and 'Hooray!' There were many hundreds of miners present. I cannot express my astonishment when I found that it was young Robert Lewis addressing the crowd. My heart gave a jump. I believed everything he said to be the perfect truth, for it never entered my head that he could be mistaken. We pushed to the front. Never shall I forget Robert Lewis's appearance. He stood upon a high mound, with a number of the principal colliers at the Red Fields Pit about him, and a tremendous crowd below. He held his hat in his left hand, and had his right extended. His eyes glowed like lamps in water, his lips trembled, his face was deathly white, and formed a strong contrast to his beard and hair as if it had been a snowball set in soot. I remember wondering why Robert's face was so pale, while preachers' faces were so red when speaking. I knew from his appearance, that every joint, bone and sinew of him were agitated right through, and I thought to myself what a splendid preacher he would have made. I had never heard him speak in public previously, and wondered where he got all those words which dropped so fluently from his lips. His audience laughed, groaned, vociferated. They were entirely in his hand. I think I could reproduce all I heard of his address …his subject was the injustice and hardship suffered by the workmen, by reason of the arrogance and incapacity of the officials. He proved, to the satisfaction of those who heard him, that the English appointees knew nothing of Welsh mining operations, that they oppressed the men and by doing so ruined relations with the masters by their conduct. At the conclusion of the speech there were loud cheers, in the midst of which I ran home to tell my mother what I had seen, what a capital speaker Robert was, and how all the people had shouted their applause. But instead of rejoicing at the news, as I expected her to do, her face assumed a serious look, which was wholly inexplicable to me.

"Well, well," she said, with a heavy sigh, "the sweet is never without the bitter. Something tells me that trouble will come of this. The day of trial is at hand. Oh! for grace to say nothing rash."

Daniel Owen was four years younger than Robert Lewis and it was wholly natural that the charismatic 20-year-old should be his hero. His own family had been immersed in tragedy, for he never knew his father and two older brothers, who had all died in a pit flood in Mold when Owen was a babe in arms. He and Robert were both marked by multiple bereavements, saw their mothers endure unbelievable hardship and carved their separate ways to fame out of their local misfortune – Robert by his oratory and Daniel with his pen. His masterpiece, "Rhys Lewis" – published five years after Robert's death – records for posterity the inspiring details of the young miner's desperate uphill struggle, his fearless stance, his balanced insights and his willingness to risk his own welfare and life itself for the people among whom he had been born.

Both Robert Lewis and Daniel Owen possessed great talents which they used to good effect, yet the sources of their skills are not readily apparent. Owen, brilliant with his pen, descended from several undistinguished generations of mining stock, and worked half his life as a tailor in Mold High Street. He was intermittently a moderate preacher, but abandoned his church work after falling ill while giving a sermon and thereafter concentrated on his writing. Robert Lewis's father, grandfather and great-grandfather did little of note except hew coal from 1750 to 1850. Talent, however, does not come from nowhere and if we trace the achievements of Robert's line of descendants we see them emerging from 19th century pauperism and acquiring a reputation in Lancashire as a solid upwardly-mobile breed of men and women lacking in neither resources, money, success nor intelligence. Robert's son Jake – a miner who broke all output records in the Wigan districts – was an individual of great stature and virility, known for his physical strength and ever-present sense of humour. The first of the Welsh Lewises to reach a reasonably old age (he died at 78) he founded a mini-dynasty of five sons, one of whom became parliamentary agent for Wigan, later being elected Mayor of the Borough in 1930 and running its finances for the next 30 years. Another son, Dick, was also a wizard with figures, while Robert Lewis III, Robert's great-grandson, was a well-known engineer. Other great-grandchildren included brilliant linguists, an IT expert and at least one world-famous author and lecturer, twice knighted in his middle age.

Robert, of lowly birth and honest, homespun philosophy, obviously passed on good genes which subsequently mingled with Lancashire ones. Not to be forgotten however are those of his stern mother Elizabeth (née Evans of Llanfair) and his Welsh wife Mary Lewis (née Hughes) of Mold itself.

Robert Lewis

CHAPTER 3

Coal throughout the Ages

The arduous, all-consuming, bitter struggle that defined the life of Robert Lewis and thousands of miners of his generation had its origins in geographical and geological developments that took place millions of years ago. Throughout his history, man has continually grappled with the planet, facing famine, pestilence, searing heat and freezing cold, earthquakes, typhoons, tempests at sea, hurricanes, tsunamis, volcanic eruptions and devastating inundations. Often he has added to his tribulations by exposing himself to dangers inherent in explorations, peregrinations, trekking, climbing, war and conquest, slavery, hunting wild animals and other perilous occupations which threaten health, life and limb. On occasion he has no choice but to engage in activity of the most hazardous kind. Coal mining is not only perhaps the world's most dangerous profession, but in 19th century Britain it was the most degrading, demoting and humiliating one. It is matched in history only by slavery, for the slaves in the galleys or the cotton plantations endured no harder toil than the Welsh and Lancashire hewers of my forebears' generation.

In North Wales and South Lancashire the formation of coal began in pre-historic times when the climate around the Dee and Mersey was much warmer than today and swamps covered much of the land.

The drier land was densely forested, and reeds and rushes grew in the shallow pools. As this vegetation died and was replaced, floods eventually covered the land and sand and mud were deposited over this layer. Over the ages the process repeated itself until layer after layer of decayed vegetable matter was compressed, under rocks, to form the mineral we call coal. Seams of coal are found in great flat sheets covering many square miles because the forests grew on flat swampy plains. The thickness of the sheets (seams) depends upon how long the forest grew before flooding took place.

Later, as the earth's crust is constantly moving, waves and folds appeared and cracks at fault lines exposed the coal. The Great Bala Fault in North Wales is an example. In the earliest days of coal mining, coal was gathered where it appeared on the surface – this was known as outcrop mining – less hazardous than working below the surface. As time went by, the realisation that huge seams existed a thousand feet or more underground led to the sinking of deep shafts and the development of 'long wall' mining along tunnels. Dangers included not only that of collapsing tunnels, but flooding (water had constantly to be pumped up to the surface), toxic air leading to asphixiation or lung damage (silicosis) and frequent explosions due to trapped gases or the use of gunpowder to bring down coal.

It is of course dark underground. In the early days, mirrors were used to reflect daylight into the pits from above. As mines got deeper, candles were introduced, but these proved too dangerous because of the gases in the workings. Many men were killed or maimed in explosions. Finally the Davy Lamp was invented, consisting of an oil-pot, bricker, gauze, metal roof and handles. Both my grandfather and great-grandfather used these (I still possess the former's). These lamps were not completely safe, for if the gauze was damaged in any way, the mixture of gas and air could ignite an explosion.

Mines contained different gases which varied greatly in their nature and degree of danger. They include, among others, carbon dioxide (black damp) and carbon monoxide (white damp). Any gas which would explode in contact with a naked flame was termed 'fire

"Rescue workers", a Victorian print from The Illustrated London News

damp'. It is found near the roofs of mines and in the pores of coal. As fire damp is colourless and tasteless, miners had great difficulties in locating it. As a boy miner, Robert remembered older men lowering candles down shafts on ropes to attract and ignite the gas, but this often caused flames to leap at them and burn their hair and clothes. On some occasions a man dressed in clothes and rags soaked in water went into the pit an hour before the morning shift began, with a candle on the end of a long pole which he used to ignite the fire damp. He would avoid the flame by lying flat on the floor while the fire damp flashed along above him. A Davy Lamp helped miners to search for the gas by using its protected flame. Fire damp was present when the flame got longer and it flickered, followed by a blue halo. In my grandfather's time, tame mice were used to detect gases.

In the 19th century, ventilation was a huge problem. Initially mines were ventilated by means of an underground furnace, kept burning near the bottom of the upcast shaft which turned into a tall chimney.

When Robert went down the pit at the age of nine, his first job was to act as a 'trapper'. This involved opening and shutting little doors, through which fresh air was sent to the galleries. Occasionally he did this in the company of girls, usually one or two years older than boy 'trappers'. Nowadays huge fans are used to cause air to circulate throughout the workings, but in the 1840s 'trapping' was a vital function during shifts and for most youngsters, like Robert, it was how they made their mining début.

Poor ventilation resulted in miners developing dust diseases of the lungs – silicosis and pneumoconiosis – and this remained a serious problem well into the 20th century. In the 1960s about 1,500 coal miners died from it every year in Britain. Robert enjoyed reasonable health as a youngster, but many children of his era grew up stunted or deformed or maimed. Illness and death came in many forms to the working classes in the industrial areas. In the year Robert was born (1832), 22,000 people died of cholera alone and in 1841 – the year he made his mining début – the average age of death of a working man in Britain was 29. The majority of these deaths occurred in industrial and mining areas such as Mold, Buckley and similar townships. The poor sanitation in the cheap terraced houses which the miners' families inhabited led to the outbreak of fatal diseases such as typhoid, scarlet fever, diptheria, tuberculosis, scurvy, malaria and infantile diarrhoea. The street in front of the Lewis's house in Garden Place was unpaved and often littered with rotting rubbish.

Children working down the mine suffered unhealthy conditions, first sitting cramped for hours as trappers (often in several inches of water) and later straining, pulling heavy tubs in awkward positions. All the time they had dust in their lungs and more often than not in their eyes, too. Hewing was of course the most exhausting task and a miner who had been down the pit since he was 8 or 9 would look worn out at 30, become asthmatic by the time he was 40 and be an old man by 50, if he survived that long. Many, including Robert Lewis, did not. Children's wages were pitifully low when Robert started. Trappers were paid only a shilling a day (5p in today's decimal system) while grown men received five shillings per day or less. In 1831 the North Wales miners stopped work, demanding a minimum wage of three shillings per day (15p), though they might only get four days work in the week and earn 60p. In 1839 (when Robert was about to start work) one estimate put colliers' wages at nine shillings a week (50p) at the most. In his first ten years of work, Robert was paid barely a half of what miners in Scotland and England were paid.

Figures such as the above have no meaning unless we take into account the cost of living for the same period. When Robert's father Jacob died in 1848, leaving Robert as the family's sole breadwinner, his wage was about £1 a week if he got five days work. My grandfather relates how this wage was disbursed:

Meat, 5 lbs	10p
Bread, 5 loaves	20p
Butter, 1 lb	5p
Sugar and tea	8p
Potatoes, 40 lbs	7p
Soap, ½ lb	3p
Candles	3p
Coal, ½ cwt	5p
Rent	15p
Schooling	3p
Other	6p
Total	85p

If Robert worked five days there was a surplus of 15p. If he worked four days there was a deficit. If he worked only three days, there would be no meat on pay day. There was another problem, too. Very often wages were not paid in full in cash, but partly in tokens for credit at the company shop. This system was known as the 'Truck' system and the shops were called 'Tommy shops'. The miner's wife was often faced with higher prices, or short measure, or both. As there was only one shop, she might have to queue for hours. If the miner refused the tokens as part payment of wages, he would soon lose his job. The system was a great source of profit for the mine owners and caused bitter disputes with the miners' families. After the 1840s, Robert campaigned vigorously against the system and succeeded in helping it to be abolished in his early twenties.

Coal mining is one of the oldest industries in the world and while the extensive deposits in North Wales led to more than a century of suffering for the Lewis family and their contemporaries, the same seams proved to be a source of enormous profits for the mine owners and the landowners who leased the land to them. Britain's huge coal deposits defined the country's prosperity in the late 18th and 19th centuries and ushered in the Industrial Revolution, which gave rise to the biggest Empire in the history of the world. The greed of the owners, investors and privileged classes increased as the industries mushroomed, and goes down in history as a cruel injustice and imposition of hardship on the downtrodden families of North Wales, Lancashire and other areas. Though disadvantaged in the extreme, Robert Lewis and his offspring played a heroic role in helping pitmen to eventually escape from their lives of drudgery, though he person-ally did not live to enjoy the fruits of his efforts.

*   *   *

Robert was barely six years old when he witnessed his first mining tragedy in all its horror. The Argoed Hall Colliery, located on the out-skirts of Mold, was a 60-man pit operated by a group of Liverpudlians called Hampton and Company. It was a small undertaking, consisting of two main shafts, the lower of which had a 16 horse power steam-driven fire engine installed to rid the workings of accumulated water. Mold at that time was in the throes of the Industrial Revolution; lead mines, a cotton factory and other pits were scattered around the hill-side overlooking the town. The Argoed Hall pit did not have a very good reputation. Children employed there worked 12 hour shifts, from 6 a.m. to 6 p.m. and were paid miserable wages. Even adults' wages were often long overdue and sometimes disbursed in low class public houses, where drinking went on and miners were known to stay all night to the great dismay of their families. The workmen had the reputation of being a rough lot, though it seems that most of them attended Chapel and Sunday School regularly.

The pit itself was a risky place. Not only was it known to be prone to flooding, but the seams were so narrow that 'young helpers' were forced to work in cramped conditions, on their knees or even on their backs.

On Wednesday 10 May, 39 workers went down on the morning shift, including 10 boys aged 16 and under. It was soon noticed that the water level was increasing, but the under-manager sent to inspect it felt things were not critical, and work progressed. Between 9 and 10 a.m. a loud rumbling of rushing water was heard and panic ensued. Men and boys ran for their lives, but soon all except five were cut off, waist deep in black water. Four escaped by swimming 22 yards, partly submerged in the black liquid; a fifth saved his life by scrambling up one of the pipes that took excess water to the surface. He ran to the colliery office to sound the general alarm.

Word quickly spread to the miners' cottages in Mold and outlying districts. Robert's father Jacob was working down another pit, but Robert ran with his mother up the hillside to Argoed along with hundreds of others from nearby houses. He knew two of the boys among those trapped – Robert and Thomas Owen – who were working the shift with their father. They were older than Robert, but attended the Bethesda Sunday school. Their younger brother Daniel Owen, who later wrote a novel about the tragedy, was a baby in arms at the time. In later life, Robert related to my grandfather his sense of horror and utter despair as he spent the best part of seven days seeing the miners' corpses, including those of the Owen boys, being retrieved and carried out from the shaft amidst the demented cries and screams of the wives and mothers of the killed. It was a defining moment in Robert's life. Though he experienced further pit disasters in the years that followed, nothing shook him so much as the Black Sunday in Argoed with its gruesome count of 21 dead, 8 women widowed and

Hungry families

30 children orphaned. Pitiful stories were related by the survivors and rescuers: John Jones and his son Richard were found in each others' arms; Robert Owen (Daniel's father) had pronounced doom on seeing his group were irretrievably cut off; on hearing his words another miner began a prayer meeting and young Robert Owen, aged 11 – 'a good singer' – led the singing. Thousands of sympathisers surrounded the pit shaft. A special non-denominational Remembrance and Thanksgiving Service was held at the Calvinistic Methodists' Bethesda Chapel in New Street. At a meeting of prominent local gentry in the Black Lion Inn, Mold, a public subscription for the relief of the victims' dependants was set up, realising the sum of £225 – 11s – 0d on the night. As Robert was to recall angrily in later years, the inquest on the bodies brought to the surface was held at the Shire Hall under Mr Parry, the County Coroner, who advised the Jury to bring in a verdict of manslaughter against the proprietors, if they

considered they had been guilty of negligence in operating the colliery. The 'twelve just men' (none of whom were miners) responded by
declaring that the employees' deaths had been accidental, caused by
asphyxia due to the inhaling of 'foul air'. They went a step further by
acquitting the owners and their officials from "any blame or neglect,
connected with the breaking in of the water". History was to repeat
itself in this regard 32 years later in the judgement on the Mold Riot
of 1869 (in which Robert was closely involved), when the authorities
were absolved of all blame in connection with the ensuing massacre.

CHAPTER 4

An Emerging Leader

By the time he was in his late teens, Robert Lewis was emerging rapidly as the natural leader of the oppressed miners of Mold and its surrounding districts. His leadership was natural, since not only was he born and bred in Mold, but he had been down the mine from the age of nine and was a fully-fledged face-worker after turning sixteen. He was strong, his output was impressive and he shirked neither hard labour nor responsibility. His very being commanded respect from every pitman, for he was one of them through and through. He led from the front and there was no doubt he spoke his mind on their behalf. Well aware of their lack of education and articulacy, he took it upon himself to be the voice of his workmates and used it with increasing ardour. The key to his ability to act in this manner was the self-education he had committed himself to from the moment he could read. It is something of a mystery that he was such a prolific reader, for his father had no such inclination, his teachers had been ineffective and his mother, above all, disliked to see him read. This was on account of his seeking out English books and newspapers, which she considered degenerate, misleading, corruptive and anti-Welsh. She herself devoured two books from cover to cover – the Holy Bible and Bunyan's "Pilgrim's Progress". She followed the edicts of the Scriptures literally and led her life in conformity with their decrees: she was a good Calvinist. Robert viewed books, especially those written in English as his route to knowledge, enlightenment, empowerment. He seems to have absorbed readily much of the wisdom they offered – his speeches were often described as astute, measured, penetrative. Reading English newspapers of all flavours informed him of current philosophies and political views and the rapid social developments outside North Wales. He became aware and was in great awe of the unbelievable rise, power and grandeur of the Victorian British Empire – the vastest that the world had ever known – its far-flung colonies and particularly its avid seizure and importation of huge quantities of the world's commodities – tea, coffee, cocoa, sugar, wheat, soya beans, seeds, rice, maize, cotton, wool, rubber, fruit, oil, gas, precious stones, ores, lead, zinc, tin, nickel, gold, silver, aluminium. And what did Britain possess to match and complement these riches, to facilitate the manufacturing that followed the Industrial Revolution? **COAL**, above all, and in large quantities. Robert perceived the huge importance of coal for the nation in the latter part of the 19th century and the centrality of his occupation, shared by his companions, in the general scheme of things. The country and the Empire derived their fabulous wealth by leading the world in manufacturing the machinery and products it needed. Great personal fortunes were made in the process. Many thousands of workers found employment in factories, mills, machine shops, foundries, forges, sawmills, all nature of sweatshops and, not least, the coal mines. In Victorian times, investors grew wealthy; workers were virtual slaves. None more so than the miners – ironically, thought Robert, since they fuelled the rest.

As Robert's horizons broadened, his perception of the blatant injustices of the era deepened. A lesser man would have lapsed into cynicism; with Robert it was more a case of righteous indignation which led to a resolve to fight iniquity. By nature he was kind and generous, but the maltreatment meted out to his community by the masters without let-up, hardened, if not his heart, his stance towards others. Where he saw bullying, hypocrisy or villainy, he flayed men with his tongue. He was only of medium height and build, but his tough, wiry appearance discouraged any physical retaliation. When he was on the rampage, men were afraid of him, even though he never resorted to violence. His rage, directed usually at officious foremen, self-important under-managers or kow-towing layabouts was all the more effective for its articulacy. As his horizons widened, so did his vocabulary, both in trenchant Welsh vernacular and frosty, rational English. His fellow miners adored him – the young ones blind disciples, the older ones gratified at finally possessing a spokesman, and a young, driving, incorruptible one at that.

His prolific reading and eager studies provided the knowledge which girded his addresses, but Robert was much more than a bibliophile – he was a born orator. He switched speaking styles at will – one moment an impassioned crusader pointing an accusing finger at the 'masters', the next serene and composed, explaining to his fellow miners their predicament, their rights, their place in the grand scheme of things – the hopes he had of bettering their lot. As he grew older he was described as a firebrand in the Lancashire coalfields, but my grandfather described the gently, soothing, reflective manner he displayed in the family circle and at smaller gatherings of Wigan miners. My grandfather was only 19 when Robert died – he often expressed his amazement at how an orator can be born – but he had the satisfaction of seeing his eldest son, also named Robert, display equal skill on the podium as Mayor of Wigan in 1930.

In later years, in his numerous speeches in the Lancashire coalfield and at other venues in the country, Robert developed a third oratorical style or technique which lay somewhere between his vigorous, recriminatory denouncements of malefactors and the soothing pacifying counsel he gave to his fellow miners. As the miners' movements in England and Wales became increasingly aware of each other and slowly gathered strength, Robert's orations took on a more didactic, constructive tone. He was not only an orator, he was an organiser. Realising that the miners' weakness lay not only in their relative

ignorance of the world, but in their lack of cohesion, he addressed more
and more the themes of coordination, unity, standing together, refusal
to yield to pressure or to abandon one's rights. In his younger days the
concept of a trade union rarely entered his thoughts; after moving to
Lancashire he began to realise that unionisation was the only solution
for miners. He never spoke in political terms; he did not belong to any
party, he had no political ambitions. In spite of his distancing himself
from politics or demagoguery he nevertheless goes down in history
as being instrumental in founding the first effective trade union in
the world, when his remarks at the conference of Lancashire miners
in Manchester in July 1869 (subsequent to the Riot of Mold) made it
clear that North Wales miners were prepared to join the Lancashire
ones in a national union. The conference deputed Robert Lewis to
establish the union, thereby designating the Manchester meeting as
the inaugural conference of the Amalgamated Association of Miners
(AAM). Though he was to be active for more than another decade,
this event can be seen as the zenith of Robert's career, inasmuch as he
had accomplished his life's goal – that of uniting the country's miners
in their pursuit of justice and release from the semi-slavery they had
endured for the best part of a century. It was not the end of their years
of oppression, but, as Churchill would have said, it was the beginning
of the end. Though he was still a semi-pauper and continued to work
ten-hour shifts, Robert was unquestionably the man the miners of
the country trusted to create their solidarity, open a path for them to
follow and begin to emerge from misery and drudgery.

*   *   *

But we are getting ahead of ourselves. In 1853 Robert was still solving
Welsh problems, and personal ones at that. Aged 21, he had been,
since the death of his father, the family's sole bread winner for five
years and though his reformist campaigning punctuated his working
week, and his interaction with workmates and overseers at different
levels intensified, he struggled to earn enough money to feed his
family. His campaigning had not gone unnoticed by the masters

and, though his prolific output of 'tubs' guaranteed him professional respect and, for the time being, tenuous immunity from dismissal, he, like other restless miners, were frequently allotted 3 or 4 days of work instead of 5 or 6. This reduction of activity meant the difference between subsistence and starvation. His younger siblings suffered from malnutrition, his mother passed up her own food to others during 'short' weeks. Robert, selfless in the extreme, was obliged to eat enough to keep up the strength he needed for hewing. It was a vicious circle for many miners – the less they worked, the less they earned, the less they earned the less they ate, the less they ate the less they were able to work. Robert frequently stuffed himself with affordable bread and dripping in the absence of meat. Carbohydrate gives one immediate energy and capacity to work hard but lack of protein and sufficient fat caused depletion of tissues, eventually weakening and unbalancing the body. Young miners, including Robert at this time, are able to withstand this debilitation for a clutch of years, but in their late twenties their health deteriorates rapidly, their resistance to ailments minimises and they die young, often in their forties, after being obliged to do less strenuous, poorly-paid jobs in the twilight of their employment.

In such adverse circumstances, Robert's mother was fortified not only by her habitual stubbornness, but by her belief in divine rule. In a sense she was nourished by her adherence to the scriptures. If Jesus had fed the multitude on loaves and fishes, she and her family would subsist on 'browes'. Naturally she resented the privations to which she was submitted; yet the strength of her religious faith made her invulnerable, short of death. She was too weak to complain, but too proud to beg. People of her ilk could not 'go on the parish' – expiration was preferable. Robert was well aware of such views, especially among women. His own hunger persisted, but increased his desperation to upset the status quo.

He was often exasperated by his mother's passive stoicism and not infrequently argued with her over what he saw as religious pedantry.

"Mother I feel as oppressed as you do by the hardships we suffer, but I'll be damned if I accept them because the Bible tells of similar privations." His mother invariably defended her views:

"Firstly it pains me to hear you use such disrespectful language. I approve of your efforts to oppose the masters, but the way forward is to maintain one's dignity in word and deed. The scriptures tell us to turn the other cheek, to forgive our fellow men, to resist the influence of Satan and to remain pure."

"Mother, unfortunately pure means poor in the circumstances we find ourselves. I neither smoke nor drink nor covet my neighbour's goods, but I find to curse a bit lessens my tension sometimes."

"When I hear such vulgar expressions emanating from your mouth, I put it down to the vile English books you read, not to anything you have heard in the House of our Lord."

"New books reflect modern ideas, my dear mother, and if we do not move with the times we and all Welsh people will languish in the backwater we presently occupy."

"I have always said that education, in our land, gets you into trouble. The pitmen, I know, are enthralled by your speeches and regard you as a future saviour, but what kind of salvation is it if you lose your job, your followers and, worst of all your soul?"

"I think you exaggerate, mother, – my rebellious thoughts and words, indeed my actions, should not offend anyone's humanity. On the contrary, if I descend into conspiracy or roughness or revolutionary behaviour it is *for* humanity and its just entitlements that I fight, not *against* it."

"I know that you are involved in a worthy cause – the good Lord knows I myself must endure the injustices you battle against – but you must find in the scriptures the noble, virtuous, blameless way to combat iniquity. The answer may be found in the contemplations of the Society, which, I notice you have tended to avoid of late."

"The Society! You know I attend Chapel with regularity and brace myself to endure week by week the inanities, hypocrisy and cant that spew forth from the preachers and some of the senior members of that institution, but to seek advice or support from that quarter in my confrontations with the masters would be an exercise of the utmost futility."

"And do you think you profit more or learn better things from the company you keep day and night down the mine, on your stump or in the pubs?"

"I can hardly not mix with pitmen – I am one myself, and in fact the fourth generation of miners since my great-grandfather Charles. I drink lemonade with those who spend most of their evenings in the pub, and whom I pity on that account. But with few exceptions I enjoy their company, below and above the surface, for they are in the main simple honest men whose cruelly prolonged and degrading toil gives them no time for idle or vindictive thoughts. Some, it is true, get sadly drunk, but even in their cups I hear less evil escaping their lips than from our pompous foremen – often English I admit – who pretend to look after us."

"I have warned you, my son, about the English."

"But even there, mother, you err. It is true that the English foremen and especially the manager – from North-Eastern England, I believe – are cold heartless manipulators with no regard for Welsh people, whom they consider inferior or mad, or worse, but the two dozen Lancashire pitmen who work side by side with us, are hardly different from ourselves. Yes, they speak in a funny manner – they say 'ah' for 'yes', 'tha mun' for 'you must', 'meight' for 'food' and 'ta-ra' for 'good-bye', but apart from that they are as hard-working, human, exploited and oppressed as we are. Like us, they bear their lot with stoicism, keep their word and have a sense of humour. They actually talk less than we do, which I think is not such a bad thing. It seems their reticence is mainly a Lancashire trait, since they say the southern English never stop talking."

"Well, I have nothing against these Lankies, as they are called, if you say they are reliable, but I would advise you to show respect for and accept guidance from our chapel members, who, as you are well aware, are at one with the miners, unlike the Church people, who look down on us."

"There is nothing in my upbringing to diminish my respect for the members of our Society, but I have to tell you Mother that in my eyes a goodly number of them proclaim to be do-gooders, but do little good, indulge in pomposity when talking to pitmen, are only too ready to speak badly of rough-looking individuals or others who like their pint, are rarely inclined to offer even the smallest financial help to cases of obvious need."

"I personally do not wish to accept charity from anyone."

"You are not starving Mother – thank God – but some people are, and I can tell you from my experience – young though I am – that the only succour paupers can expect or receive in their desperate plight – comes from the poorest sources – the pitmen themselves, including a few of the Lankies who happen to have some extra pennies."

"I can see that my advice and example hold little sway with your opinions, my son. I can only pray that Our Father will look kindly on your actions and keep you in His fold."

"Don't worry, Mother, you will never have reason to be ashamed of me, but I will have to follow the dictates of my conscience – that is the way I am made. It cannot be the wishes of the Lord to see the poor pitmen of Flintshire and their families endure indefinitely the misery and malnutrition that is our present lot. One day He will change our lives for the better and where and when I can help Him to do this, I shall be there."

Such utterances approached blasphemy in the ears of Elizabeth Lewis, and their arguments continued in this manner from the time of her husband's death to the fateful days of the Riot of Mold. In spite of their different interpretations of good and evil, they loved each other possessively. In a few years Elisabeth married a second time, to Robert Savage, another miner of Mold. Her son, Robert Lewis, 'emigrated' to Wigan with his family in 1856, but they remained close all their lives and his visits to Mold continued up to her death in 1873 and indeed his own in 1880.

CHAPTER 5

Dismissal

During his last few years in North Wales, Robert became an increasingly painful thorn in the side of the Leeswood Colliery's managers. Most days at the end of a shift he would make his way to a mound near the pit-head, black-faced, clogs on his feet, lamp in hand, and squat, collier fashion, on his haunches and wait for pitmen finishing their shift to gather around him. These were *ad hoc* encounters, unlike the more formal addresses he gave every week or so. The miners, many of them squatting around him, told him of the state of the face they were working on, relating any accidents (falling coal, loosening props, random flooding, accumulations of gas, jammed tubs, minor injuries) that had taken place in the preceding hours. Such accounts were routine – pits were scary places. Falling coal inflicted many face wounds – bruising, bleeding, broken skin, perhaps broken noses. A miner who suffered a bleeding face in mid-shift would rarely go to the pit-head to have it seen to – it could incur walking a mile. Mostly, they dabbed at the wound with greying handkerchiefs, staunching the flow of blood but failing to prevent coal dust getting under the skin. Most pitmen, including my grandfather, had a network of thin blue lines all along the bridge of their nose and often on their forehead and cheek-bones.

Other more serious matters would be brought to Robert's attention: ailing children, under-nourished grandmothers, drunken brothers, nagging wives, leaking roofs, mounting debts. Robert knew only too well the depressing effects of the hardships they described – he had his own fair share of them at home – but he gave counsel in a calm, sympathetic manner, sharing their misfortune, but not their anger, helping where he could, consoling where he could not. It is remarkable that older men, some of them in their thirties and forties, perhaps fathers of half a dozen children, would seek out this compassionate, composed twenty-year old to unburden their woes. They listened to what he said, trusted his advice, looked up to him. Robert for his part did not like them to fuss over him. After half an hour he would pick up his lamp and slip away home, hoping that his mother had scrounged a few vegetables somewhere for their evening meal. After eating, he would light two candles and in their flickering light he would read the day's newspaper, if Elizabeth had not hidden it.

In clement weather his meetings would be held in the open air in different parts of the town, sometimes near the railway station, in front of the chapel, on open ground behind pubs or, more provocatively, near the pit-head. On occasion, mine officials and foremen would join the meetings, standing well at the back, never interrupting. Miners often looked back at them, glaring contemptuously, but Robert kept a grip on his audience at such times and there was no violence. Though the officials did not dare to interrupt or question Robert, he frequently addressed them directly or indirectly, in parts of his speech. He did not hesitate to confront them with the harsh facts of the life of pitmen in Mold. The coal market was brisk (he was able to give statistics) but where did the profits of this booming industry go? Why do our overseers and the greedy strangers who accompany them eat like lords, fill our pubs and strut in their finery at week-ends, while miners' families remain half-starved, grateful for the odd scrap of meat to go with their bread and potatoes? Why, when we go with our miserable pittance to buy enough food to keep us alive, must we even then fill the masters' pockets with the revenue

Before the shift

from your hated 'Tommy shops'? Yes, we can go farther afield to buy food, but men whose wives have dared to do this have lost their jobs. Their families, deprived of the aforementioned pittance, have been thrown on the parish and suffered that humiliation to add to their gnawing hunger. Do we live in a free country where we can shop where we want, say what we wish, choose our means of livelihood? Is a pitman inferior to a farmer, a carpenter, a boiler maker, an engineer, a teacher, a churchman? Are our children of less consequence than those whose fathers stand at the back of this meeting? Do they have gruel at bed-time as ours do? Do miners not contribute enough to the national well-being? Is our coal, which we extract so laboriously and at risk of our lives, of no value to our famous industries? Welsh coal powers our railways, our factories and furnaces, our steam-engines, the handsome ships which patrol the shimmering seas of our glorious empire. Is slavery abolished or do black faces in Africa and North Wales serve their masters as in days of yore?

Often, when Robert pitched his remarks at this level, officials would sneak away, surreptitiously, without looking back, though miners noticing their departure would sneer openly at them and hurry them on their way with phrases not heard in drawing rooms. Robert never commented on their retreat, he lacked vindictiveness. Ignoring their departure was the best way to add to their shame. Most of the surreptitious onlookers were indeed guilty of shame; they had either been sent by their superiors to spy and report back on the miners' activities or to hear if they themselves were vulnerable to some future attack. To infuriate them more, Robert spoke half of the time in Welsh, an incomprehensible medium for the English among them. At certain times the management had attempted to forbid the use of Welsh in the mine – a clear indication of their sense of insecurity. Occasionally a foreman or some official would show sympathy for the miners' plight, but did little to help them materially, as each feared for his own livelihood.

Robert, in his speeches, exhorted the pitmen to better their conditions and he continually insisted that wages had to rise. It was only common sense that malnourished workers would not be able to increase production. This was a problem which was not solved for another two decades in Wales, and even reductions in wages took place at certain times. The other topic close to Robert's heart was the safety (or lack of it) of his fellow pitmen. He had been irrevocably scarred by his witnessing the Argoed disaster and fatalities still occurred at regular intervals in the mines of North Wales and other parts of the country. Courageous though he was, he dreaded the prospect of being crushed, killed or maimed himself, since he was only too aware of the utter despair it would bring to his defenceless family. His addresses, especially when there were 'spies' present, frequently referred to the dread that gripped the humble rows of miners' cottages when the news broke of a roof fall, an inundation, an explosion, a closing of an escape route, where men – fathers, sons, brothers, uncles – would be crushed, drowned, maimed or, worst of all, trapped to be asphyxiated over a number of days. Those who had a family member on the particular shift would rush in a panic to the pit-head, be aghast at the recovery of a corpse of a loved one, stand in anxious vigil night and day for trapped ones – return in inconsolate despair to their bereaved homes if the worst had happened – widows, orphans, fatherless or otherwise devastated, facing an unforgiving future even more cruel than the bleak past.

A master of pathos, Robert described these tragedies with tears in his eyes, but his self-composure never deserted him. He lived in sorrow, but never in despair. His exhortations to the miners did not include incitement to violence. He did not speak of strikes, though they would clearly be a weapon. Strikes were regarded as unpleasant – an English phenomenon foreign to Wales. Welsh people would settle their differences and rectify their inequalities and injustices through discussion, debate and common sense. Alas, they did not know the nature of the Victorian English Establishment at whose hands the workers of Northern England also suffered ignominy. Robert in later life was obliged to link striking action with protest, but it was for him a last resort, short of violence. It was probably his mother's view of morality that induced Robert to believe that calm endeavour and simple honesty would ultimately triumph over meanness and greed. This conviction never deserted him completely, though his brushes with the masters, backed by the 'authorities', not to mention the 1869 massacre of Mold, brought him ultimately to confront reality, sharpen his attacks, lead in person rebellious marches, relish his conflicts with the courts of the realm, ally himself closely with the Lankies, instigate the formation of an organisation which made its mark in English (and Welsh) history.

*   *   *

One of the difficulties facing Robert was sporadic, unruly behaviour on the part of a clutch of his fellow pitmen. Such were the injustices of the age and the rough-and-ready nature of some miners who endured them, there was bound to arise untenable situations where something had to give. Robert's reforms were steady but slow, as reforms often are. He had got the management into a corner over the Tommy shop issue. Promises had been made to lower the prices of some basic commodities and dismissing men whose wives shopped elsewhere was becoming less acceptable for the shop-keepers. In principle wages

were being reviewed, though officials dragged their feet. One afternoon an under-manager named Stirrup upbraided half a dozen men
who had gathered at the pit-head shouting protests in Welsh and subsequently cursing him in more understandable English. He unwisely
swore back at them and a couple of the more hot-headed ones decided
it was time for him to leave town. Though he did not know it, it
was a well-worn Mold tradition to "run somebody out of town",
not in the cowboy manner with horses and gunshots, but in equally
effective measure where the victim is carried bodily to the railway
station, provided with a one way ticket to some unsavoury destination
(e.g. Liverpool?) and bundled onto the train with a few belongings
snatched from his house. The hapless Stirrup had been carted half
way to the station under this arrangement by the six men in question,
followed by a cheering bunch of miners who had been made aware
of the event, when a couple of constables – also alerted – intervened
and tried to extract the under-manager from the rebels' grasp. An
unresolved struggle ensued lasting 15 minutes or more, the gaggle
gradually closing in on the station, when Robert Lewis arrived on the
scene, attracted to the event from his nearby cottage in Garden Place.
He attempted to placate the rebels, whom he knew well, but for once
they over-rode his advice. At this point one of the constables snatched
Stirrup momentarily free, while another pitman knocked down the
other policeman. Robert Lewis got between the fallen bobby and his
assailant and after a lot of pushing and shoving fell down himself, but
managed to drag himself and the fallen law officer to a nearby piece
of grass. When two more constables appeared on the scene, Stirrup
was eventually released, his 'bundle' was restituted and two of the
hot-heads and Robert Lewis were summarily arrested for disturbance
of the peace.

This was the first of several nights that Robert passed in Her
Majesty's prisons, though he was never detained for more than one
night at a time. This was just as well, as there were ample witnesses,
including one of the constables, to affirm that he had not initiated the
action. His mother had of course thrown a fit on hearing of his arrest,

but was mollified by the constable who had been partly trampled on and who went round to her house to assure her of a quick release.

Robert's reaction to the event was immediate and of a furious nature. His anger was directed not at the police or even at Stirrup. He declared at a meeting he held near the station the next day that the six colliers were culpable. Emphasizing how hard and how long he had supported their cause, how he was prepared to sacrifice his own job and well-being to snatch them from the degradation they endured, he condemned without reserve their actions as stupidly irresponsible, as being entirely retrogressive for the cause they were all fighting for. He foresaw vindictive retaliation on the part of the management, aided and abetted as usual by the Flintshire authorities. His forebodings were only too true, as his own working week and those of the rebellious six were slashed mercilessly in the following months, and survival on the resulting reduced income became critical. His mother admonished him for getting involved with the outbreak – admittedly he had not approved of it, but his speechmaking and reforming zeal had undoubtedly been contributory to the clash. He found it hard, for once, to contradict her.

*   *   *

The following year was a difficult one for the Lewis family. Not only was the reduction in working hours making it almost impossible to make ends meet, but the police, at the authorities' bidding, started to clamp down on Robert's meetings. These had grown in size after the Stirrup incident; Robert was regarded even more as a heroic leader and the management became increasingly nervous of his influence with the men and the impressive size of his audiences. Again, Robert's plans were hampered by the more volatile of the pitmen, and several of his meetings featured chaotic shoving and occasionally brawling. On principle he withdrew from rowdy gatherings – they contradicted the rational, honest-to-goodness atmosphere he was able to create – but the police were slow to distinguish between his role and that of his audience. When chaos ensued, they began to arrest him to preserve the peace. Robert of course 'went quietly' on such occasions. He would not sponsor rowdiness (which inevitably led to violence) and there were times when his removal from the meeting was the quickest way to achieve quiet. However, he got sick of being arrested. He was always treated well, for the police themselves considered him a kind of folk hero (they were simple men themselves), but regular arrest was no fun for Robert. The food in jail was more substantial than at home, but that was poor consolation for being deprived of his family's company and affection. He decided he could not continue living like this; he must either change vocation or location. There was no way he was going to abandon his reforms. The alternative was to 'emigrate'. He loved his native North Wales but the prospect of seeing the lovely scenery too often from behind bars lessened his appreciation of it. He must go elsewhere, out of reach of the Flintshire authorities. Emigration meant England, the northern part for sure. He knew a couple of pitmen who had gone to Wigan and found work there. Mines were plentiful in South Lancs, and the wages, though derisory, were marginally higher than Welsh ones. He seriously began to consider the possibility of pursuing this plan.

*   *   *

Three events accelerated his decision. The first one was the re-marriage of his mother who had become increasingly morose of late. At 51 she was no longer young and had lost her physical attractiveness, partly due to the inadequate diet she had subsisted on for many years. But in mid-century Mold and especially in the working classes, people did not marry for love or beauty or even sex. Security, friendliness, compassion were what counted and Robert Savage, an eligible bachelor at 39 – twelve years younger than Elizabeth – fancied the rather stern, upright character that Elizabeth presented to the world. He asked for her hand. She had no reason not to offer it. He was a miner, a kind soul, and revered Robert Lewis. An extra wage would not be unwelcome in the household and if things were a bit crowded, that was the norm in miners' cottages.

The second event which changed the fortunes and composition of the Lewis family was Robert falling in love. At 22, he had all the healthy, natural inclinations of an extrovert Welshman and when Mary Hughes, his 21-year old sweetheart, announced she was pregnant after a whirlwind courtship, Robert had no hesitation in doing the right thing and they were happily married in the glorious month of July 1854.

The house in Garden Place was not quite bursting at the seams, but if one of the happy couples decided to move on, it would solve more problems than it caused. Elizabeth was more than capable of looking after the younger children – young Elizabeth aged 16 (she died at 18) and Edward and John, 14 and 11 respectively.

The household increased by one in 1855 when Robert Lewis's son, John, arrived on time. Mary was delighted and was keen enough on Robert's plans to move to Wigan where she imagined she would be able to run a house of her own.

*   *   *

The third event that hastened Robert's departure from Garden Place was the most compelling: the colliery sacked him. His dismissal had been on the horizon for some time. He had never been given an ultimatum, either orally or in writing, but Robert had sensed that the termination of his employment was imminent. In the last few months, mine officials who earlier had been willing at least to argue and debate with him had granted him fewer hearings. True dialogue had ceased; the masters had heard enough of what he wanted to say and, in all truth, were adamant in their refusal to meet any of the miners' demands. Robert Lewis was dangerous for them; they wanted him out of Mold, out of North Wales if possible. It was unlikely that Robert would find work in any other mine in the neighbourhood. The owners closed ranks in such cases.

Another half dozen pitmen were 'given their cards' at the same time. They were ones viewed unfavourably by the management for one reason or another. All of them had attended Robert's meetings, two of them had been in the habit of complaining vociferously, even during shifts. One of the quieter ones was Thomas Hughes, Mary's younger brother and Robert Lewis's brother-in-law. In addition, another of Mary's brothers, Edward, aged 14, too young to be a face worker, was told he needn't come to the pit – his job had been given to another lad. It was bleak news all round in the Lewis and Hughes households.

The families conferred for several days. All were agreed that refusal to leave would get them nowhere – neither was it possible. No one except Robert knew the law and he advised against hiring a solicitor to claim wrongful dismissal. They had no money to pay a lawyer, there was no legal aid at the time; those who were seen as part of the Establishment were regarded as invulnerable. Robert was now determined to leave for Wigan. Not only was he confident of gaining employment in this most prolific of mining areas, but he sensed he would be in a better geographic location to reach a significant body of mine-workers who had the rugged character – and the numbers – to help him realise his aims. Lancashire miners totalled tens of thousands, they were unhappy with conditions and they were already in contact with thousands of pitmen in Staffordshire and the size-able mines in Yorkshire, Durham and the North East. Robert was bi-lingual and had already spoken to miners in South Wales as well as throughout Flintshire. Once the Wigan pitmen learned to trust him and give him a base, he could see his way to uniting the great majority of the nation's mine workers. He had never been to Wigan, though the people there had heard of him. He would have to start at the bottom and achieve recognition the hard way. Wiganers, he knew, were a tough, wary crowd. He would have to dig deep in more ways than one. When a month later he stepped off the train in Wigan's bleak Wallgate station, little did he know that in 70 years time his grandson, Robert Lewis II, would be mayor of the Royal Borough of Wigan.

The two families agreed on the course of action. Robert would go to Wigan and look for work; he would take his two brothers-in-law,

Thomas and Edward Hughes with him. Though little more than youngsters, they were hardened pitmen. Mary and one-year-old John would stay behind until they had found suitable lodgings. His mother and Robert Savage assured him they could manage on Savage's wages for a few weeks. Once Robert and his brothers-in-law started earning, they would send money back to help.

CHAPTER 6

Destination Wigan

*"Deep in the mines dense gloom profound, far from the suns
bright ray, under the safety lamps pale gleam, the miner toils"*

Inscription in the stained glass window in Wigan Town Hall

Wigan is only 35 miles from Mold as the crow flies. Robert Lewis knew personally half a dozen Welsh miners who had left the Mold area to find work in South-west Lancashire. After his own 'emigration' in 1856 hundreds of pitmen followed his example to find employment in Wigan and its satellite districts of Ince, Hindley, Ashton-in-Makerfield, Billinge, Garswood, Haydock, Orrell and Pemberton. It was not only proximity and availability of work that influenced Robert's selection of the royal Borough of Wigan as his next sphere of activity. It was a prudent choice for additional reasons.

As early as 1725 the celebrated writer, Daniel Defoe had visited Wigan during his travels around Britain and had commented specifically on the excellence and particular characteristics of the local coal:

"In the neighbourhood of this town is found that kind of coal they call Cannel (or candle) coal, which though found in great plenty, and very cheap, is yet very singular, for there are none such to be seen in Britain, or perhaps in the world besides. The coals so soon take fire, that, by putting a lighted candle to them, they are presently in flame, and yet hold fire as long as any coals whatever ... They are smooth and slick when the pieces part from one another, and will polish like alabaster ... a lady may take them up in a handkerchief and they will not soil it, though they are as black as the deepest jet."

This coal was often referred to by other observers as "black marble" and many attractive objects could be carved from it, such as salt-cellars, stand-dishes, snuff boxes and miniature statues. The presence of this type of coal, in great profusion in this part of the Lancashire coalfield, was a happy accident of fortune waiting to happen; it foretold wealth, for somebody.

Wigan centre

Wigan Pier

The River Douglas, flowing through Wigan, became navigable around 1720 and the Mersey and the Irwell were made navigable as far as Manchester around the same time. Wigan, situated almost exactly halfway between the Manchester and Liverpool metropoles, was emerging as the natural geographical hub for coal production and its transportation. The Sankey Canal, in around 1760, provided the important Haydock Collieries with a waterway. The invention of the steam engine (by Watt in 1784) and its fuelling requirements, signalled the commencement of coal mining to rank in importance as one for the greatest industries of the country. Landowners lucky enough to have coal beneath their lands leased mining ventures left and right. Robert Lewis, with his experiences in Wales, was well aware of the plenitude of royalties which accompanied such good fortune.

He was also aware that such fabulous mineral riches, in due course, must benefit those whose hard labour and physical skills were the real engine room of the wealth. Mining expertise was developing in Wigan as early as 1792 when Walker's *Tour from London to the Lakes* refers to Dick Melling's bucket engine draining valuable cannel mines; he comments on Wiganers' mining skills and powers of invention. The miners themselves were beginning to realise their importance within the industry and in the context of their positioning in the plethora of different industries dependent on coal. The first Wigan miners' strike, though short in comparison with later ones, took place in 1792; Robert knew that some organising groups of miners had held secret meetings in the Goose Green area. What clout the Lancashire miners had (less significant in North Wales) was the huge dependence of many nearby industries that sprang up leading up to and during the Industrial Revolution. A French industrialist, J. Dutens, visiting Wigan in 1819 and describing the mammoth coal seams encompassed by Wigan, Leigh, and Chorley, stated that the industrial complex "was the biggest and most important operation that has ever been formed in a country." This was no mean boast. The importance of coal mining as compared to other minerals in Lancashire by the mid-19th century can be seen in the total annual value of real property in the country assessed in the year ending 5 April 1843. This amounted to £7,756,228, of which £4,777,536 was for houses, £1,636,416 for land, £39,728 for tithes, £593,515 for railways, £71,590 for canals, £348,007 for mines, chiefly of coal, and £21,038 for quarries; the remainder of the sum being for other miscellaneous forms of property.

This assessment, and others of the same nature, were current at the time Robert Lewis envisaged making Wigan his home and place of work. His own efforts were reinforced by the long-established mining genius of Wigan leading to the setting up in the town, one year after his arrival, of the first purely coal-mining college in Britain (1857). The significance of this institution – known as Wigan Tech – was one of the reasons Wigan would later become *the most important coal-mining district in the world*, known as "Coalopolis".

The output of coal in Lancashire in 1874 – a year in which Robert Lewis's trade union activities were at their peak (he was indicted for leading "riotous processions") – was 16 million tons from a total of 558 pits. Thus we see how in a period of 18 years Robert had advanced from his lowly station as a lone, downtrodden defender of the rights

Blundell's Colliery, slag heap

of a few hundred tyrannised and half-starved colliers in Flintshire, to be a key representative of a labour force in England and Wales that actually produced four-fifths of the world's coal as well as more iron than the rest of the world put together.

But we have to turn back the clock, for in 1856, when Robert went to look for lodgings in the Ince district of Wigan, a bleak and hazardous fate awaited him. The coal mines of south-west Lancashire were known as the most dangerous in Britain. The high rate of mortality in the Wigan area was due to the exceedingly gassy seams and poor ventilation systems which led to a spate of violent explosions between 1850 and 1854. The pit where Robert happened to find a job, Ince Hall Colliery, had suffered two disasters within one year; on 24 March 1853, fifty-eight men and boys were killed, while on 18 February 1854, a sickening total of 89 perished. The deaths were the result not only of initial explosions, which instantly killed about half the men, but of asphyxiation and poisoning by inhaling afterdamp as air failed to circulate through disrupted ventilation. When Robert started his first shift as a face-worker in this ill-fated pit, memories

were still fresh from the 1854 disaster; his unease on hearing accounts
of it from fellow-workers was far from lessened when they informed
him that one of the colliers who had been killed was a certain Robert
Lewis, unmarried, aged 22 from Wigan, born in 1832, the same year
as Robert Lewis of Mold.

CHAPTER 7

Moving House

Robert and his two brothers-in-law, Thomas and Edward Hughes, were met at Wallgate station by Jack Johnson, a Lancashire pitman five years older than Robert, who had done a two-year stint in Mold a few years earlier. Johnson knew Robert well – he had attended several of his meetings and had kept in touch with the young Welsh orator after returning to Lancashire. When Robert wrote to him regarding his move to Wigan, he offered to find lodgings for the trio and take them there to inspect them on arrival.

Finding accommodation for a pitman's family in Wigan's working class districts in 1856 presented little difficulty, as the frequent mining disasters caused dozens of widows to vacate their houses and go and live with relatives to save costs. After the 1853 and 1854 Ince Hall explosions, Ince, particularly, had vacant dwellings. These were in rows of terraced, blackened brick houses, laid out in grids, forty to an acre. They were all of the two-up-and-two-down variety, usually straddling the collieries themselves. Nearly all were company-owned – the average rent was five shillings a week.

Johnson knew of an empty house at Sally's Gap, 100 Warrington Road, in Ince. This was about one mile from the station and Johnson had thoughtfully brought along a wheel-barrow to transport the

Welshmen's five suitcases which contained half the Lewis family's belongings, including pit clothes and equipment. It took them about an hour to reach the proposed dwelling, one of three houses known as Rock Farm, though the farmyard had ceased to exist.

Number 100 presented no surprises to Robert, used to similar houses in Garden Place. The front door opened onto Warrington Road itself, paved long ago but with numerous pot-holes. Behind the row were the 'backs' – an unpaved alley, dusty in summer, a sea of mud in winter. As in Garden Place, this area served as a play-ground for children. Parallel to the houses was a row of lavatories, one per house; washing lines criss-crossed the area; one tap served the street, two wooden buckets stood beside it. The midden trenches ran under the line of lavatories – they would be emptied once a week by the 'muck-men', who usually worked in pairs. One would shovel the muck and the other do the cinders. It was normal for them to alternate in these tasks, often quarrelling about whose turn it was to do what. All household rubbish, including human waste, found its way into the midden trenches – when they were emptied on Fridays the smell lingered till the following Tuesday. Each toilet seat was a wooden board with a circular hole in it. It paid to keep plenty of cinders around. There was no water, gas or electricity in the houses in those days. Lighting was by candles or paraffin lamps.

Robert did not demur at what he saw. Choosing a house was not difficult, as they were all the same. He went from room to room for a look round. The house had been empty for three months – the walls were covered in grime. Upstairs were two bedrooms, one slightly bigger than the other. Of the two rooms downstairs, one was the 'parlour' – the front room – the one at the back was the 'kitchen'. The kitchen, with bare flag-stones was the living room used for sitting, dining, cooking and washing (in a big wooden 'dolly' tub). Next to the tub was a smaller galvanised bucket which served as an indoor toilet. The parlour, with its cheap lino, had a battered sofa, a low wooden table and two upholstered chairs that had seen better days, and years. Miners used parlours so infrequently that they were practically

A miner with his lamp

wasted space. They entertained rare guests on Sundays, Christmas
and birthdays. They were full only at weddings and funerals, when
often the coffin would be stood up in one corner to maximise room
for the mourners. Lack of space led to miners sharing beds, those
returning from night shift taking the still-warm places of those going
on morning shift. In big families it was not unknown for individuals
to sleep a day or two alongside newly-deceased relatives until a coffin
had been procured.

Robert's practised eye noticed the cracks in the brickwork caused
by subsidence (the workings of the mine would be right under most
of the houses). He also took in half a dozen cages stacked in the backs
near where the cinders were collected. He suspected these were for
pigeons (most pitmen were pigeon fanciers) and for ferrets miners kept
to catch rabbits, to supplement their diet. "I guess it'll do," he mut-
tered to Johnson, well aware of his urgent need for shelter (that very
night in fact). Johnson assured him that he would get work within a
week, such was the shortage of experienced hewers in Ince Hall. The
two young ones unloaded the suitcases and took them upstairs. There
were no beds but the versatile Johnson promised them three mat-
tresses later in the day. They had brought blankets and clean sheets
from Mold. They would not stay clean very long, but Mary would
come in a week or two and organise things. She had a cot for infant
Johnny. For a couple of years Rock Farm provided ample space for the
small Lewis family. It would grow in due course.

*   *   *

The next day, Jack Johnson took Robert and his two companions
to the offices of the Ince Hall and Cannel Company's Arley mine,
located to the east of Britannia Bridge off Warrington Road, half a
mile from Rock Farm. Arley was desperate to sign on face workers and
quickly enrolled Robert at a daily wage of 4 shillings (about sixpence
more than the Lancashire average for hewers). Thomas, the elder of
the Hughes brothers, was taken on as a drawer at three shillings a day
and Edward, 14, as a lasher-on at two shillings. Shifts were nine and

a half hours. Derisory though these wages were, Robert found it hard to hide his satisfaction at his quick turn of fortune, as he had earned nothing for over a month. Immediate employment meant he and the boys could raise the money to bring Mary over within a matter of weeks.

The following Monday they all went down on the morning shift. The shaft was 414 yards deep, the seam they worked on was four feet high. Lighting was relatively poor, but Robert noticed how the Wigan cannel coal was much shinier than the coal he had hewed in Wales. In two weeks, when they were paid their first wages, they had settled into the Arley routines. The best news was that they had to walk only 800 yards to the pit shaft and a mere half mile to the face. The memory of the two recent disasters, however, weighed heavily on their minds.

*   *   *

Mary, little Johnny and four more suitcases arrived at Wallgate station one month later. Robert Savage accompanied them; Jack Johnson's wheelbarrow was drafted into service; it was a Sunday bright and sunny. Wigan smiled on their reunion and when they had enjoyed a meat and potato lunch, Mary unpacked and embarked on the task of making Rock Farm liveable. The Hugheses were a house proud family – more than the Lewises of Mold had been. Mary set about her task with energy and enthusiasm. The building and environment offered few possibilities – it was in every sense a humble dwelling – but it was Mary's first home of her own and according to my grandfather Jake's account, she did a good job (he spent his first 20 years there). She had brought with her a lot of her 'tranklements' from the Hughes household – plates, glasses, Toby jugs, two mug dogs, a huge barge tea-pot, various brass cups and candlesticks.

The back place, or living room, had a decent-sized fireplace with a red-brick 'crow' upon which one placed three pans. Most of the modest cooking was done in cooking pots, the oven being used for puddings, pies and cakes (rarely affordable). To make room for pots and kettles, a four-barred 'luby' could be hooked onto the front of the hob. In the centre of the hearth was a brass plate called a 'duster' or 'tricket' which was taken off every morning in order to remove the old ashes. 19th century heating was of course by coal fire. Cleaning out the 'hess' was followed by whitening of the hearth area with chalk and mops. A Welsh brass fender fenced off this area. Every Friday morning the whole fireplace had to be blackened and polished up. This was known as "black-leading the grate". At the same time all the brass parts of the fireplace would be polished as well as all the other brasses such as the Welsh candlesticks, brass cups, ashtrays, poker, fire-tongs and shovel. Friday was also the day when Mary cleaned the windows, changed the lace curtains she had brought with her, whitened (with rubbing-stones) the door-steps and flags. The Cornish, or mantelpiece, was lined with an array of pewter jugs, candlesticks, large canisters for tea and coffee. All these objects were dusted and cleaned weekly. The room also had a chest of drawers on top of which was a white linen cover with crochet work (Mary's mother's work) round the edges. The family Bible lay in the centre of the linen cover and had a lace cover of its own. This was also changed every Friday. Friday was quite a day.

The neatness and orderliness, not to mention cleanliness, of Mary's home was sabotaged every day by returning miners, black-faced and covered in coal dust from head to foot. The men stripped down to their underpants and plunged up to their necks in the dolly tub hot water, provided by dozens of kettles boiling on the hob. The flag stone kitchen floor would be flooded twice daily as the pitmen soaked, splashed and scrubbed themselves. After a year or two most miners' skins said goodbye to whiteness. They settled for a light grey, adorned here and there with thin blue lines where coal dust had got under the skin when it suffered cuts during a shift. Few miners could be bothered to dress a wound during a hewing session. Other miners detested bathing in hot water at all (there was a belief that it was bad for the back.) Such men would get into a dolly tub once a week or once a month. They were of a darker hue than some of their companions.

Robert was a regular bather, though there were occasions when he flopped down exhausted after doing overtime and had to be awakened around six to eat something.

Mary invested in a green plush sofa for the parlour, which eventually boasted two mahogany rocking chairs, a square walnut table, a chest of drawers and a small china cabinet containing a selection of Wedgwood plates and a couple of Welsh love spoons. White lace curtains draped the windows. There was also a yellow blind, as was the fashion of the time. Two paintings of young women graced the walls. One was called 'Sally in our Alley' and the other 'Black-eyed Susan'. After a while Mary covered the cheap lino with red and green matting.

The two bedrooms each contained a double and a single bed. There was no room for other furnishings. Bed clothes were changed once a week and stored under the beds. Coal was kept under the stairs. Monday was washing day in the backs – a chaotic jungle of props, pegs, clothes-lines, pit drawers, vests and shirts; sheets billowing like spinnakers in the Lancashire westerlies, grey suds, coal dust and wild-eyed housewives everywhere.

CHAPTER 8

Settling Down

In 1856, when Robert Lewis ceased to be a Welsh miner and became a Wigan pitman, the industry in Lancashire in general was in a sorry state. The consecutive disasters at Ince Hall Colliery of 1851, 1853 and 1854 had left the pit and its immediate vicinity in turmoil. The death total of 160, creating more than a hundred widows and hundreds of fatherless children, was all the more devastating since Dickinson, the mines inspector, had told the Select Committee on Mines in 1852 that Ince Hall Colliery had one of the best sets of safety regulations in the whole country. He hoped other collieries would model their rules on them. The subsequent inquiry revealed that the workers themselves had broken the regulations in various ways, letting the furnace, necessary for proper ventilation, go out, leading to the major explosion. Such negligent behaviour was not uncommon among Lancashire miners, who often disregarded menial procedures in order to lighten their labour.

Robert had noticed, when working side by side with 'Lankies' in Wales, the rough, uncompromising streak in their character. They quarrelled little with their Welsh fellow-pitmen, but could be vicious in their attitude towards the masters. Now, in Wigan, Robert was confronted with the full potency of the miners' irascibility. Wigan pitmen, angry and half-starving, had no hesitation in reacting with violence to their luckless, often desperate plight. Due to the hazardous nature of their work, they were openly contemptuous of danger and, being extremely tough, were unafraid of physical encounters. Such men, in considerable numbers, represented a formidable foe for the forces of law and order. If their demands were flatly rejected and where their union did not have the funds to sustain a prolonged strike, they would take to the streets, mob-like, engage in ubiquitous fist-fights, attack property and sabotage machinery. Such aggression had a long history even in other parts of Great Britain. In 1757 when the price of corn rose steeply, "an insurrection of the colliers" in Bristol led to the city being occupied for two days.

The Lankies in Wales had told Robert of a particularly vicious struggle which had taken place in Wigan in 1853. The Ince Hall explosion in March had set everyone's teeth on edge and when the colliers' request of an increase of two pence in the shilling was refused, 5,000 men came out on strike; a week later a similar rejection to the textile workers resulted in a total of 13,000 men and women striking in the town. Violence erupted in October when the coal owners, meeting in the Royal Hotel, turned down a further request. This led to a peremptory assault on the hotel. Nine constables, arriving on the scene, were greeted with a hail of potatoes, apples, oysters and tomatoes (colliers' sense of humour) and an hour later the pitmen controlled the town. Public houses, the town hall, the post office and the grammar school were all seriously damaged, as were the police barracks in Millgate. Wood was ripped from the market stalls and a home-made bomb blew off the roof of the engine-house at Moss Hall Colliery. Only when Captain Gerrard and the Lancashire Hussars arrived was order restored. After that the Mayor of Wigan admitted that a turbulent town of 35,000 could not be controlled by nine policemen (who themselves only earned about 18 shillings a week).

The *Manchester Guardian*, though criticising the Mayor, had a few unkind words for the pitmen whom they described as "monstrous nuisances and pitiable mistaken creatures". They went on to say "The

Wigan coal-miner is possessed of some idea of the permanent value of his order. Without those large bones and thick sinews of his, he thinks that every art and business must come to a standstill; and from thence it is but an easy transition to suppose that his class will always retain the power of reducing the world to capitulation."

Robert, who rather fancied this interpretation, rejoiced in the awareness that now he was among a community of men and women who had the courage, sense of purpose and stamina to realise, in the not too distant future, the aims of reform that he had longed for, in less propitious circumstances in Wales. The Lancashire colliers, however, though determined and vigorous, were little better off materially than their Welsh counterparts. In Mold Robert had had to eat 'browes' to survive; in Wigan the equivalent was salted potatoes, or oatmeal and boiling water. Cases were reported where people exhumed buried cows to eat their carcasses. Hunger was a constant companion of both miners and their families. David Swallow, a Yorkshireman who organised the Miners' Association in Yorkshire and later in the Durham area, made this plea to William Hulton, a mine owner at Westhoughton near Wigan: "We ask for a raise on behalf of our once-blooming but now hunger-stricken and emaciated wives and children; we ask it for ourselves who have to descend every morning in the pit, without breakfast, so you can grow rich while we sink by slow degrees into a premature grave, victims of over-exertion, nauseous gases and starvation." Swallow, whose orations straddled the Pennines, echoed to an uncanny degree the speeches Robert Lewis had made in Flintshire. Both men, pacific at heart, agitated less out of political convictions than out of sheer distress over the inhuman privations suffered by their class and families. Robert had considered conditions in Mold were rock bottom, but he soon saw that Wigan miners faced roughly the same fate. The Lancashire death rate due to accidents in pits was twice the national average. At any one time colliers filled two beds out of five in Wigan Infirmary. Miners' longevity was 26.1 years, compared with 34.2 years for agricultural workers and 34.0 years for other labourers. A pitman obliged to seek relief from the Poor Law Guardians received eight shillings and nine pence a week (based on five children). If he worked hard (full time) in the pit he would get three pence extra. Swallow, who was often prevented from speaking in the open air, just as Robert Lewis had been in Mold, decried the unbelievably low pay – "Who would be a collier to be exposed to an hourly death; to have his head split in two; his brain dashed out; and all for sixpence a day." Robert noted that women and children too were no better off than in Wales. Women, chained and belted like animals, dragged large loads from the depths; for hauling three tons of coal to the surface, they were paid one penny. Little children, often younger than those, like Robert, sent down the mine in Mold (some of them were five and six years of age) often fell asleep as they toiled for up to eight to ten hours in cramped underground conditions. In 1853, after seven weeks of strikes and empty stomachs, hundreds of men, women and children were forced to go from house to house in the Wigan districts of Ince, Pemberton and Orrell, asking for alms. Magistrates tried to stop the begging. Many families were evicted at the same time from their cottages and strike-breakers were brought in from Wales. Robert had seen that Wiganers, like his mother Elizabeth, were often insanely proud and he understood fully the depth of despair that had obliged them to go begging.

*   *   *

It was not long after his arrival in Wigan that Robert was sought out by William Pickard, the local miners' agent. Pickard who was born on 10 February 1805 in Burnley, had, like Robert, been sent down the mine at the age of nine to support his mother and two younger children (he had been made fatherless at the age of three). Though twenty-seven years older than Robert, he had heard of his orations in various parts of North Wales and welcomed my great-grandfather eagerly to join him as a speaker in Wigan and surrounding districts. Pickard was a father-figure for Robert for the next 20 years. The two men, though of different generations, had a lot in common. Apart from having almost identical family situations, their views on the miners' plight and perspectives on the whole industry coincided completely. Both were willing to devote every waking hour to attempt to rescue their fellow pitmen from their drudgery and privations. They were uncompromising in their attitude to the masters: injustices must be remedied; wages must be raised to enable people to live decently; safety and welfare must be prioritised. Unlike some unionists, they were not implacably opposed to everything the masters did. Pickard, in Lancashire, had experienced many occasions where owners had recognised that their interests often

William Pickard

coincided with those of the workers; explosions devastated everybody; undernourished men could not maintain productivity; gases, faulty ventilation and flooding were recurring calamities that had to be eliminated; safety procedures and better equipment must be provided; above all the masters must display basic humanity; the alternative was increasing conflict and ultimate ruin for all. Pickard was of the opinion that if agitation was kept within reasonable bounds, if fair play was the objective of negotiation, if miners' violence could be minimised, then colliers could capitalize on the strong cards they held in their hands – the insatiable demand for coal fomented by the Industrial Revolution – and the rapid mushrooming of a whole variety of industries in south-west Lancashire. Robert, always a moderate, agreed fully. He saw clearly that the Lancashire miners (and Wiganers particularly) were much better placed to improve their lot than his fellow Welshmen had been. Apart from the economic and geographical advantages of the area, the critical question of transporting coal was being solved by the rapid development of local waterways. Wigan cannel coal was of a better quality than that mined in Flintshire and the densely populated Wigan hinterland provided the weight of numbers to apply pressure on coal owners and landowners alike.

*   *   *

In the second half of the 19th century, Wigan was the coal capital of the world. South-west Lancashire had the fastest-growing population in the country and the concentration of mines, ironworks, textile mills, canals, navigable rivers, ample labour and the nearby metropoles of Liverpool and Manchester, made Wigan the hub and centre of gravity of mining activity. Yet trade unionism had been slow to develop in Lancashire. There were various reasons for this. Though mines were numerous – 100 in Wigan alone – many of them were small-scale units, perhaps employing 20 to 50 men. The dispersion of pitmen caused them to focus on the problems of their own workings instead of acquiring wider perspectives regarding the industry as a whole. Small units made it difficult to create a centralised organization. Miners drank and socialised with their mates and there arose a conglomeration of small separate unions, independent of each other and with specific local aims.

A noteworthy characteristic of most Lancashire miners' unions was the rivalry between them. They were sometimes slow to help a neighbouring union in financial or other type of difficulty. By contrast, miners' unions often showed solidarity with unions in other industries (e.g. textiles) and frequently came out on strike with them. Robert felt that Welsh miners had been more closely knit, though less courageous and aggressive. He was astonished at seeing bitter disputes between coal owners themselves. Apparently they had been going on for centuries. The lack of solidarity between the different Lancashire districts constantly hampered Robert, as one of his objectives was to encourage people to resist in unison, not only in South Lancs but also together with colliers in North Wales and Staffordshire – his main areas of activity.

Coal owners also delayed the progress of trade unionism, through what might be described as judicious paternalism. Most mines were small and the owner knew all his men personally. There were often mutual ties of loyalty between master and servant. Those men who wished to better themselves quickly took advantage of what was known as the "butty" system. A butty was a kind of chartermaster, who would be appointed by the master to supervise production. Butties were generally unpopular among miners, as they had benefited from favouritism and earned more money. The system created divisions among the workers and in itself militated against trade unionism. Robert, who had suffered at the hands of overseers and intermediaries in the Leeswood Collieries, generally ignored their influence, though their existence continued for many years more. My grandfather Jake (Robert's son) always spoke scornfully of them. The butty system died out in the 1890s.

Another method used by the masters to control labour mobility was the 'bonding system'. This was a contractual agreement which bound a miner to work for the coal owner for a given period, e.g. one or two years. They would be paid two or three shillings on signing the agreement, but would forfeit a large sum if they absconded before completion. This feature restricted the miners' choice of work and employer considerably. In the Durham area this system persisted well into the 19th century. In Lancashire, many miners absconded and sought jobs elsewhere. In the Wigan area, where mine owners were in constant competition with each other, switching employers was easier than in other coalfields. This was one of the reasons why Robert Lewis, known to be a skilled hewer, found little difficulty in getting accepted in Ince, though it was no secret that he was no longer welcome in Wales.

*   *   *

More than a quarter of a century before William Pickard, Robert Lewis
and Thomas Halliday inaugurated the Amalgamated Association of
Miners in Manchester, an organisation called the Miners' Association
had been formally established in Wakefield on 7 November 1842. It
lasted only seven years.

Initially, it promised much. It certainly represented an advance on
previous combinations of workmen and could claim to be national
inasmuch as at its peak it had a membership of nearly 100,000 and
had 98 lodges in Lancashire and Cheshire. It influenced legislature,
particularly that pertaining to Lord Ashley's 1842 Bill prohibiting the
employment of women and small children underground. It employed
a famous solicitor, William Roberts, who fought many legal battles
for the miners in Lancashire. David Swallow, the general secretary,
expanded the association's activities from Yorkshire to Durham and
the North West.

Unfortunately, for most of the decade the union was riven by disputes. Lancashire had the largest membership, but the pitmen there
were the least cautious of all and conflicts with mineowners were
bitter and constant. The latter retaliated against the workers' demands
with mass evictions, legal attacks and importation of large numbers
of Irish strikebreakers. Outsiders, hungry for jobs, had little sympathy
for striking Lankies. Finally the masters smashed and beheaded the
organisation in December 1848, when 76 of its prominent members
were arrested and jailed at the South Lancashire Winter Assizes.

*   *   *

In 1856, when Robert Lewis joined forces with William Pickard,
the Miners' Association was a thing of the past; the Amalgamated
Association of Miners lay well in the future. The hotchpotch of
unions and lodges in the Wigan area, not to mention those in Wales,
the Midlands and elsewhere, cried out for leadership and a strategy
of unity and coordination to evade and escape from the divisiveness
of the previous decades. Robert, though a fiery speaker, had always
stood for moderation and cooperation between different miners'

units. Pickard had the same inclinations. Other miners' leaders such as Halliday and Thomas Oakes of Hindley were much more militant.

Though Robert Lewis and William Pickard had somewhat different priorities, they had a common view of the miners' grievances and predicament. They can be summarised as follows: the employment of boys under 12 years of age was illegal, but still widely practised; women continued to slave away underground and "ont' pit brew" (there were 500 in Wigan alone, earning 2 shillings a day); hours of work were cruelly long (in winter many men saw daylight only once a week on Sundays); wages were paid only fortnightly (this led to drunken orgies); lack of legal rights (in disputes, most magistrates were coal-owners); lack of education for miners and their families; unfair weighing of coal; inadequate number of inspectors leading to breaches of safety regulations; obligation for miners to buy supplies in company stores; arbitrary laying off of pitmen at the employer's whim; lastly, and most importantly, the derisory level of wages.

William Pickard was a powerful figure in union affairs, being the miners' agent for Wigan, Pemberton, Standish, Aspull and Blackrod. He concerned himself principally with the legal rights of miners and the machinery of arbitration, the plight of female and under-age workers, problems relating to their restricted opportunities of education, the miners' hours of work and how remuneration was calculated. Robert Lewis's chief preoccupations were miners' safety, (which involved him with the organisation of the Wigan Miners' Provident Benefit Society); the coordination of union activities in Lancashire and North Wales; filling the role of 'permanent agitator' – giving orations in a variety of locations (Bolton, Burnley, Manchester, Wigan, St. Helens, Burslem, Wrexham, etc.); organising and leading miners processions; chairing the Weighing Committee of the West Lancashire Coal Trade Association; workers' compensation in the case of fatal or near-fatal accidents; the cost of miners' supplies at the tommy shops.

Both Lewis and Pickard agitated continually for higher wages. Thomas Halliday – more militant than either and constantly involved in miners' strikes – concentrated on attempts to establish central control of union wage bargaining. All three men were dissenters (Pickard and Halliday had been Methodist lay preachers). During one dispute with coal-owners, Halliday was constrained to retort that the miners' leaders were not "a lot of broken-down teetotallers and Methodists."

Such was the background of the Lancashire mining industry and Robert Lewis's fellow-unionists, when he began a gruelling 24-year stint as a face-worker in Wigan and district pits, following each shift fulfilling his duties as miners' agent, conference delegate, orator and agitator. He was also the father of a growing family, all the members of which finished up down the mine or in Ince cemetery. Let us follow his (often tragic) life and progress in the next chapters.

CHAPTER 9

Nobody can be Late

R obert's work routine at Ince Hall was relatively simple, as he lived near the mine and did not need any transport. Some miners had to walk miles to the pit shaft (later they came in trams). Arley was only half a mile from Rock Farm: Robert got up at 5:30 and ate his breakfast – usually bread, cheese and two cups of tea with plenty sugar – until 6:00. He would make his packed lunch (in Wigan they called it 'jackbit') – sugar butties (once a week bacon butties) – which he put in his tommy tin. Dressed in his pit clothes – vest, coarse short jacket and trousers, thick woollen socks, clogs and flat cloth cap – he clattered his way over the kitchen flag-stones and left the house at 6:10 to present himself at the lamp room to register and collect his safety lamp just before 6:30. It may come as a surprise to some to learn that pitmen are the most punctual of people. As one hundred men may be going down in four cages simultaneously, anyone coming late might miss the shift (also a day's wages) – a catastrophe for his household.

Robert would be at the pit shaft at 6:30 and down at the bottom at 6:40. He would then walk half a mile or so (the coal face might well be under his own house) and start work at 7 a.m. He would hew continuously till 2 p.m. with a ten-minute break for jackbit and tea or water at noon. After that, clearing up, helping his drawer, other minor tasks might take 30-40 minutes. He would reach the surface about 3 p.m. and hand in his 'tallies' [1] showing how many tubs he had filled. Miners often squatted around the pit-head and exchanged remarks as they drank more tea. It was normal for him to get home by 4 p.m. and immerse himself in the dolly tub for 20 minutes, followed by Thomas and Edward (same water) if they were so inclined. For the first three months they worked the same shift. Soon after, Thomas graduated to face worker and they worked different hours, which didn't make life any easier for Mary, who spent many hours fetching and boiling water and mopping flag-stones.

Working conditions, Robert noticed, were as cruel, if not more so, than in Wales. He felt particularly sorry for the boys – some as young as seven or eight – who would often start work without having breakfasted and sip a cup of water with a slice of bread in mid-morning. Coal dust often made it difficult for them to swallow their miserable sandwich; older men learned to suck a piece of cannel an hour before eating, to produce some moisture inside the mouth.

Some parts of the pit were extremely hot, men related seeing candles melt and losing nearly a stone in weight (14 lbs) during a shift. 'Thrutching' was unbelievably hard work on some of the steeper slopes and many adults and even boys showed hair loss above their foreheads through pushing the tubs with their heads. Women, too, were engaged in thrutching and hauling (chained to their tubs). Females underground were much more numerous in the Wigan districts than in Wales or the Manchester area, where the 1842 Act forbidding the employment of women below the surface was more strictly observed. For pecuniary reasons Wigan coal-owners flouted regulations and between two to five hundred females were active in Wigan in the 1840s and 1850s. Masters posted look-outs to give warning of police

---

1. Each collier had a set of "tallies". These were metal strips with a number punched on them and a bit of string attached that would be threaded through a hole in each of the tubs the collier filled. The drawer would check these at the top and when they had been counted would take them off and take them down again the next day.

Alexandra pit

approaching to apprehend women on the job. Many women were dressed as men to avoid detection. Robert had experienced Welsh women's aversion to underground labour, but in Lancashire many females were opposed to the ban and worked in a clandestine manner when opportunities arose. He never fully got used to the sight of these amazons clad in rough mens' jackets and trousers and short petticoats, their legs enclosed in stockings without feet, called 'whirlers'. When thrutching, the women would have a belt round their waist and a chain passing between their legs as they hauled their loads on hands and feet. Many were pregnant and the belt and chain became increasingly irksome; some worked right up to giving birth. Both children and women were often beaten by drawers. Maltreatment of mine children was widespread; supposed delinquents were punished according to barbarous rules. They could be caned mercilessly on their bare posteriors with thin pieces of wood, if they dared steal a pit dinner or fail to keep pace with their duties.

The youngest children, from seven to nine years old, were normally employed as 'trappers', opening and closing brattice doors to regulate ventilation. Though trapping was possibly the least strenuous of pit jobs, it was also in a sense the most wearying and pitiable, since a child might sit 12 hours in the dark, cramped and stiff. At times when waggoners did not pass through it was solitary confinement of the worst order. For this, boys got 5 shillings a week. Many fell asleep on the job and were sometimes half carried out by their fathers. It was not infrequent to see the youngest boys carried down the pit on their fathers' back – in a way, they were the lucky ones. Hungry children often ate candles and vomited.

Arley mine was a 'hot' pit and gas was the principal cause of the disasters that had occurred in previous years. Robert was astonished at the recklessness of some of the Wigan pitmen whom he saw working in gas until almost unconscious, so unwilling were they to lose a day's pay. Other Wigan pits, like those he had seen in Wales, had 'wet roads' where working in black water gave miners boils, rheumatism and chronic inflammations. In such pits water would often cover clogs and men and women would wade their way to the face. Worse still, where water-logged workings combined with extremely low seams men could not even crawl and had to 'swim' along the floor in six inches of dust-laden water, dragging their picks and shovels as best they could. A mid-century report on conditions in Lancashire mines stated that "the hardest labour in the worst room in the worst conducted cotton mill is less hard, less cruel and less demoralising than the labour in the best of coal mines." While Robert fully agreed with this interpretation, he also knew that abuses in cotton mills were more flagrant than in pits. It was known that some children were compelled to work at their looms from six in the morning until midnight and were beaten with knotted ropes if the master was dissatisfied with their work. There was little doubt that morale among Wigan miners was significantly higher than that of textile workers. Colliery owner William Hulton of Westhoughton (hardly the most benevolent of masters) declared in a report to the government "it is

Underground in a Wigan mine

incredible to see the difference between the comfortable state of the miners in Westhoughton and the misery of the hand-loom weavers who live 'over the hedge.'" There, half of the 5,000 inhabitants were totally destitute of bedding and nearly so of clothes. Six per cent were in a state of famine. Robert Lewis was later to have altercations with William Hulton; nevertheless he knew that miners' spirit, both in Lancashire and Wales, could never dip below a certain level of dignity and sustainability. Whatever the deprivations of pitmen might be – and they were considerable – the elite, the colliers themselves, remained the aristocrats of hard labour. He was convinced that they would ultimately triumph.

While the average height of Lancashire coal seams was four feet, others could be as low as 18 inches; men suffering from claustrophobia were unable to work these. Robert was slightly claustrophobic, though his son Jake was not. Whatever the height of the seam, falling lumps of coal could be lethal, depending on their size. When a man was killed in this manner, he would be dragged out from under the rock and carried out of the pit as soon as possible. News of his death would spread rapidly to the other lanes and it was a tradition for all miners to down tools and abandon the shift as a sign of respect.

Often, though not always, pay would be deducted. In any case it was the custom for the pitmen to make a collection for the widow – whatever they could afford. Coal owners never paid any form of compensation for a miner who died, while working, of natural causes. If death was a result of injury, the amount paid depended on the relationship between the owners and the workers. There were some instances of masters showing generosity to the dependants of pitmen who had enjoyed mutual loyalty with the owners. Other cases were brutal in their stinginess (and widows could be evicted from their cottages a few weeks later!)

Eventually the Fatalities Scheme, introduced many years later, gave dependants a more reliable benefit. One of its conditions was, of course, that after a fatality the men should remain at work. The tradition of respect, however, carried on for many years. Compensation for miners was one of the things that Robert Lewis focussed on during most of his career, so shocked had he been at an early age by the Argoed disaster. He had heard that in Yorkshire coalfields, pitmen often 'died twice'. When someone was a heart attack victim during a shift, his fellow pitmen, for the sake of the man's wife and children, mutilated the body with falling coal so that they would qualify for compensation, however small that might be. Robert had not heard of such cases in the mines he worked in, though "what passes underground in the dark tunnels in which men toil is little known, even to the overlooker." Some real accidents were truly frightful. After Robert had been in Wigan a few weeks, one unfortunate pitman had his head caught in a drum-shearer and was literally 'scalped'. Such gory details were always hidden or withheld as much as possible from enquiring wives.

*   *   *

"Arley Mine", The Illustrated London News, 9 April 1853

During his first few months of shift work at Arley, Robert Lewis, witnessing Wigan mining life and conditions at close quarters, was able to take stock of the situation and draw comparisons with the scene in North Wales. While he was increasingly excited at the possibilities that the adventurous and resilient character of the Lancashire pitmen opened up, he found little cheer in their current plight. If one took the death rates as the closest approximation to being an objective criterion, Wigan was the most unhealthy town in the British Isles. The Board of Health regularly issued statistics for 50 towns in England and Wales and most years Wigan topped the list in terms of vulnerability. In 1858 Wigan's death rate was 42 per 1,000, as opposed to the national average of 27. The borough's high mortality rate could not be attributed to an ageing population, since Wigan had the highest birth rate – 53 per thousand against a national average of 33. It was certain that the high death rate, partly a result of dirtiness of houses and lack of sanitation, was largely due to the inverse longevity of miners and their dependants, who averaged a life span of 22 years!

Mining, along with deep sea fishing, was obviously the most dangerous profession to follow. While falls of rock, toxic gases leading to explosions and frequent flooding were the main hazards faced by pitmen, the chronic development of lung diseases like silicosis and pneumoconiosis shortened workers' lives, as well as outbreaks of cholera and diphtheria that plagued Wigan throughout the 19th century. Even Wigan people outside the working classes did not enjoy a normal life span. In mid-century masters and senior managers connected with the local mining and textile industries had an average life span of 38 years compared to the national average of 52. While mine and mill owners and landowners with mineral royalty rights amassed great fortunes as coal fuelled the Industrial Revolution, not all of them prospered continuously. A Lancashire proverb says "Clogs to clogs in three generations." Robert heard of Thomas Darwell, a Wigan cotton mill owner, whose Sovereign Mills made him vastly rich and enabled him to live in Ince Hall before becoming Mayor of Wigan in 1823 and 1830. Shortly afterwards, his business crashed and, at the time of Robert's arrival in Wigan, Darwell died in poverty in Patrick's Row, a working class area of the town.

Robert perceived that Wigan pitmen were more reckless than their caution-inclined Welsh cousins and his tidy mind disapproved of the way Wiganers disobeyed safety regulations, worked in extremely gassy conditions (often rashly exposing flames "to see better"), shunning helmets of any kind, preferring wooden pit props to the more efficient metal ones (which were heavier to carry) and showing scant respect for female co-workers whom they periodically battered and occasionally impregnated. The desperation was similar to that of the Welsh miners but its sequel was visibly more barbaric. Nevertheless he was consumed with desire to help pitmen of all colours, smarting with the knowledge that 7,000 privileged individuals owned four-fifths of the British Isles. The colliery owners at least risked their money, though they exploited the workers ruthlessly. The landowners with royalties amassed riches and did **nothing**. But in moments of calm he reckoned that time was on the pitmen's side. More and more cotton and other mills created an insatiable demand for coal. Transport was less of a problem, for *the mills had come to the coalfields* – the momentum was unstoppable. He hoped he would live long enough to witness the reversal of fortunes.

Chapter 10

Life at Rock Farm

*"It contained several large streets all very like one another
and many small streets still more like one another inhabited
by people equally like one another, who all went in
and out at the same hours, with the same sound upon
the same pavements, to the same work, and to whom
every day was the same as yesterday and tomorrow, and
every year the counterpart of the last and the next."*

Charles Dickens, "Hard Times"

Meanwhile, Mary Lewis was trying to come to grips with Wigan. One could say she was trying to cope with double culture shock, firstly adjusting to the environment and secondly to the nature of its inhabitants.

In the time of the Romans, Wigan was an important Roman military encampment, known as Coccium. It was situated on the Roman road leading north through Chester and Warrington. The town has its place in history: it was loyal to the King during the Civil War of the 17th century. Indeed, the Royalist cause in Lancashire sustained

its final defeat at the Battle of Wigan Lane. Earlier, in 1246, Wigan
had been granted its first Royal Charter, making it one of the four
oldest boroughs in Lancashire. At that time, Manchester was only a
nearby village!

The four principal streets of Wigan – Wallgate, Standishgate,
Millgate and Hallgate – are a legacy of Scandinavian settlement in the
10th century. 'Gate' means 'street' in Scandinavia even today. Besides
dominating the coal industry, Wigan was the most important centre
after London for pewter for several centuries. It was also well-known
for its manufacturing of grandfather clocks, bells and crossbows!

These past glories were no longer visible when Mary Lewis was
set to appraise the borough in 1856. Already a hundred years before,
the famous Methodist, John Wesley, had described Wigan as "a town
proverbially famous for all manner of wickedness." A Victorian writer
saw it as "a place of mental barrenness, where ignorance and vulgarity
are their boast, and literature has scarcely dawned." This was probably an exaggeration conceived by an Englishwoman who did not
understand the workings of a Wiganer's mind. Mary, however, when
enquiring about security, was told that a few years before the entire
Wigan police force (six men) had been sacked for being drunk.

Warrington Road abounded with noisy pubs, but these paled into
insignificance in comparison with the rowdy drinking houses of the
Scholes, a two-mile-long street across the River Douglas, which in
1860 boasted 60 pubs (Wigan had 300 in total). The Scholes, knocked
down in the 1960s, was the prototype of an industrial slum, consisting
of a thousand mean miners' cottages, packed side by side, climbing
a mile-long slope of blackened cobbles punctuated here and there
with pot-holes, nettles, yellowish-green sods and last night's debris
from the public houses. Rock Farm was 15 minutes walk from the
Scholes, which Mary visited most days on account of the convenient
little corner shops there which sold food and life's other necessities
at rock bottom prices. She never dared venture into the area at night
as rambunctious miners, downing countless pints of beer, fell out
of doorways, celebrating goodness knows what, but always ready to

A street in the Scholes

accost or engage anyone in a skirt or to attack individuals in trousers they did not know or did not like. Police patrolling the Scholes had difficulties every Saturday night clearing the colliers out of Scholes public houses, such as the Crofter's Arms and the Windsor Castle: it was not unusual for 40 or 50 people to have to be dragged out at one or two o'clock on Sunday morning. Once on the street they were most "turbulent and riotous", using blasphemous language ("By the heart of Christ, I'll tear thy liver out"). When they were bound over by the magistrate to keep the peace, Scholes pitmen would break it at once. Penalties had no effect, as they would club together, raise money and pay the fine immediately. Quite often they would be accompanied in their debauchery by their wives, who were equally blasphemous and quarrelsome. Even children of twelve or in their early teens would often be seen drinking and smoking with their fathers.

Sally's Gap at Rock Farm was considerably less tempestuous and lawless than nearby Scholes, but for Mary it compared unfavourably with the poverty-stricken but relatively unruffled Garden Place of Mold. In North Wales one could look out on serene green hills. Wigan's equivalent were the slag-heaps, symbols of a town in the process of disembowelment, not an aesthetic scene. At first the ugliness of Wigan's back streets repelled the Welshwoman. Mines and pit heads she was used to, but Wigan had symbols of ugliness in profusion – clustered round the volcano-like slag heaps were mineshafts, piles of industrial waste, chimneys, mills, glassworks, chemical works, factory-sheds, canals, flashes, railway shunting lines, all interspersed between grids of tightly-packed terraced dwellings housing 120 people per acre.

The density of construction did not bother Mary so much – closely-packed rows of houses were a feature of Mold, too – but in Wales you

Scholes' Rows

A view across the Scholes

could see where houses began and ended, you could see **green** as well
as bricks, you knew when you were leaving one town or village and
entering another. In south Lancashire, from Wigan to Warrington
or Burnley or Ashton-in-Makerfield it was one huge congeries of villages, thickening ever and anon into towns, seldom thinning out into
anything that could be called country. The unplanned, unhealthy and
utterly unlovely towns were thrown up with scant or no regard for the
people who would have to live in them. Such was the rapid development of manufacturing in the mid-19th century and the hurried need
of accommodation for the workers at the heart of it. At that time if
one drew a circle of 20 miles radius with Wigan as the centre, the
total population inside it exceeded one million. It would have been
hard to find anything comparable, either in England or Europe.

Mary – houseproud as she was – felt she could do something with
her four rooms and privy. The temporary adequacy of accommodation
had served them well – Jack Johnson had spotted the opportunity. It
was well-known that in the Scholes and other parts of Lower Ince and
Pemberton some families lived 10 in one room, often sharing it with

animals. With Mary cleanliness was a fetish. She and her brothers scrubbed every inch of their grimy walls. They found they could never let up with dusting and wiping: coal dust penetrated every nook and cranny. The smoky squalor seemed natural to Wigan pitmen – coal was used daily for domestic purposes – the concessionary variety that miners were able to obtain cheaply was dirty by comparison with the shinier cannel. Steam engines by now had become ubiquitous in Ince and Wigan, contributing, along with belching factory chimneys, to the continual pollution of the atmosphere.

The air had been a lot better in Mold, yet Mary noticed that Wigan pitmen hardly ever complained. Inured as they were to often-choking conditions underground, they did not demand exacting standards above the surface. Men constantly coming in and out of the house with dirty clogs and apparel, not to mention dolly tub activity, gave housewives little respite. Of more concern to Mary (and indeed Robert) were the want of sewers and drains, the lack of refuse disposal, the difficulty in fetching water and getting it to the house clean, the poor ventilation of the upstairs rooms. Robert working full shifts and attending meetings most evenings, could hardly help with maintenance. Yet Mary, who lived at Rock Farm 17 years and bore seven children there, succeeded (according to my grandfather Jake) in running a household that was pleasant to live in and be brought up in. The effort, however, probably contributed to her early demise – she died at 37 years of age.

Mary's decent, almost decorous, household was matched by few others in Lower Ince. Her neighbours, paupers like herself, struggled less to maintain appearances. Few of the other houses in the row had chairs. Miners were in the habit of squatting for long periods or sat on clogs. Large families stood in a circle round the table at mealtimes. Some people used orange boxes to sit on, eventually chopping them up for firewood. Coal kept under the stairs often spread over some of the flagstones. When concessionary coal ran out families would augment their supply by going out 'coal-picking' round the slag-heaps. Many houses had walls leaning at different angles due to

Wigan Pit Brow Girls.

subsidence. The walls of most cottages were so thin that you could hear every word of the conversations of the neighbours on both sides. Children whose parents did not swear learned curses from the folk next door. Mary, brought up as a strict Calvinist in Flintshire, was appalled at the amount of swearing that went on in Wigan. Robert, frequently out of love with Welsh chapel-goers, swore occasionally for effect when in a fiery mood, but my grandfather Jake, who was the toughest pitman in Wigan and district, never used any bad language, so Mary had obviously taken pains with his upbringing.

Many of the neighbours' children were in a pitiable state. Deprived of sunshine through long hours of work underground, they were stunted in growth, pale of complexion, often mean and hungry in demeanour. Mary would see boys and girls washing together in open doorways, boys often naked and the girls with almost nothing on but a shirt and an under-petticoat. Usually they washed their faces and ears but rarely their bodies; you could see a ring round their necks after washing. In the evenings most miners and their wives would go to the pot-houses and the younger children were often left to fend for themselves. Some would come round to Mary's door. It was not their custom to beg, but the Welshwoman always had scraps to give them.

Several of the pit-lassies in the row had bastards – even some of the married ones. They rarely exhibited any shame in this regard and often seemed proud of an illegitimate child if it was good-looking. None of the bastards were treated worse than the other children. As in Wales their schooling was minimal – most of them were claimed by the pit at the age of eight or nine. The majority remained illiterate (like their parents) throughout life, though those whose parents sent them to Sunday school were taught to read and write. In the 1860s and 70s the Free Churches and the Roman Catholics built schools as best they could and Robert and Mary's children benefited accordingly, though their first-born Johnny, born in Wales, missed out on literacy.

The younger boys in the row all wore woollen jerseys, usually red or grey in colour, with short trousers held up by braces. Long grey

The Scholes on a sunny day

stockings and clogs completed their attire – few wore any underwear. Older boys, like their fathers, seemed to wear pit clothes all the time. Pit-brow lassies wore long, coarse dresses reaching well below their knees, revealing six inches or a foot of thick woollen stockings and clogs. All wore big headscarves, some men's trousers under their dresses. In winter they often slept in the same clothes for two or three days at a time, especially when half a dozen of them shared a room. Upstairs rooms smelled of unwashed bodies. Cottages were supposed to be whitewashed every five years or so. Some remained untouched for 10 or 15 years.

Mary was used to witnessing poverty – it was endemic among the miners' families in Flintshire. Though wages were higher in Wigan, her neighbours seemed worse off than in Wales. This was partly due to excessive drinking, but also to what many considered improvidence. The fortnightly payment system caused pitmen to run up debts for two weeks, so that the earnings of each reckoning served only to pay off the debt that had been incurred in the previous fortnight. Thus families were permanently in debt and accordingly the best customers of the pawnbrokers. Whatever 'best clothes' they had, they kept at the pawnbrokers during the week and took them out on Saturday night to wear on Sunday and then take them back again on Monday morning. It was recognized that higher pay (a collier's) did not mean his family would be better off than other classes of workers. Farm labourers seemed to manage better on 12 shillings a week than pitmen on 20-25 shillings! Miners of course normally worked under agreements with masters and often could be laid off a few days for one reason or another. If this happened too frequently, the pitman's debt would rise to unmanageable proportions and he would have nothing to collect if he had only put in eight or nine days work in the fortnight. On such occasions the masters used to lend men money to stabilize their account. The loan would then be paid back in instalments. It was a classic vicious circle of poverty.

Mary's moral upbringing hardly led her to approve the miners' habits on Sundays. If the weather was good, some couples would take two gallons of beer with them and bask in the fields while consuming them. Many pitmen spent Sundays poaching and bird-catching. Other leisure sports were whippet-racing, cock-fighting and even linnet-singing matches, all of which involved betting and often loss of income. Another Wigan speciality was the holding of 'Pastry Feasts' in local pubs from the Scholes to Goose Green. These were primitive beauty contests where courting couples paraded in front of drunken miners, who accorded them varying degrees of approval and not a few bawdy comments. The most attractive girl received a prize of a pint of rum and a sixpenny pastry, whilst the girl adjudged least attractive (ugliest) won a pound of black pudding.

Such relatively harmless pastimes, though disastrous for pitmen's wives' budgets, often smacked of humour and engaged sporting instincts. One Wigan 'sport', however, horrified Mary in the extreme. This was the practice of 'purring' sometimes defined as "the Lancashire method of duelling by clogs". This was fighting in the raw, where two men, usually miners, kicked each other with their clogs until one fell down. He would then be kicked continuously until he was senseless or, in not a few cases, dead. 'Purring', like boxing, was carried on for money. Spectators bet heavily on the outcome. In cases of deaths (there could be two or three a year) or maiming (a dozen a month) 'victors' were sentenced from anything up to six months or 15 years in prison. In Wigan and surrounding villages responsibility for such outrages was often laid at the door of the police, who were either too weak numerically or in calibre to tackle the vicious pugilists (brawlers, duellers). Lancashire police had a bad reputation in mid-19th century. They assaulted and arrested each other, wrote out false expense claims, stole beer from the Wigan Brewing Company, got drunk while on duty, molested women who turned to them for help and were regularly sacked by the authorities to be replaced by unlovely recruits who rarely lasted in uniform for more than six months. Mary gave policemen in Warrington Road a wide berth; neither did she trust other officials after she heard of two miners and a woman going to the office of a Wigan registrar for one to sell his wife to the other for the sum of 4 shillings and sixpence. The official let them "sign their hands to a bit of paper" which, in their ignorance, they believed would make the transaction lawful.

During the day, Mary observed many boys, ages ranging from eight to twelve, who only went down the pit on certain days, as now and again even their fathers would be laid off. These part-time pit-boys did not, however, go to school on days between work. Truancy was rife in Ince and a local clergyman estimated that out of 1,500 lads who should have attended school, only 1,044 actually did. When Mary asked her neighbours why they did not oblige children to go to school when they were laid off, she found little enthusiasm among the parents. There existed a belief that if boys were not introduced to working habits until they were 12, they would develop an aversion to toil that would mark them for life. Mary objected to such an opinion and succeeded in getting Jake into Sunday school long enough to enable him to read and write. But it was a close thing, as both he and Johnny started as trappers at nine and a half. Robert, already in

Wales, had determined to do all he could to keep his children out of the mine, but when the time came, their wages, paltry though they were, were needed to keep them all from starvation.

But that was a few years later. On arrival in Ince Mary had only one-year-old Johnny to look after, though she was expecting again at the beginning of 1857. There was no question of her having to work and her brothers were paying their way. Many of the other women in Sally's Gap, however, were working, several as pit-brow lassies. A process was underway to get women working underground to transfer to the surface (to comply with the law). Two of them were trained as engine-drivers, pulling wagons loaded with coal from Winstanley to Wigan Pier. Unfortunately the experiment, though well-meaning and progressive, was less than successful as the new drivers knocked down a small child (compensation £1-10s) and later struck a cow crossing the line (compensation £10).

Over the next 15 years, Mary would see schools and better housing emerging in the ravaged districts of Ince, Aspull, Blackrod and Haigh. Lord Balcarres, the most enlightened and beneficient of the local colliery owners, built decent houses such as Top Row and Cut Row, to serve the workers of Arley Colliery. Methodists, Baptists and the unions all played their part to raise the pitiful standards of education in the Wigan area. Religious and schooling needs were catered for by a school and a mission hall under the wing of Upholland Parish and the Primitive Methodist Chapel in 1870. Lord Balcarres built schools at New Springs and Red Rock in 1875. The adjoining ancient parish of Standish and its daughter parishes of Shevington, Coppull and Charnock Richard, built schools and churches that greatly helped to dispel ignorance and brutality there.

But these developments were in the future. In 1857 Sally's Gap and Rock Farm were in for some hard times.

CHAPTER 11

The Era of Disasters

On 23 January 1857 Mary gave birth to a son whom she and Robert promptly christened Jacob, after Robert's father, who had died nine years earlier. The infant appeared somewhat of a weakling, no doubt due to the poor diet that Mary followed, but the renewal of grandfather's name in the family was a source of rejoicing. The new boy arrived a month before little Johnny's second birthday. The members of the household doted on infant Jake, and his two uncles helped Mary with his care in the evenings, as Robert was often out of the house at meetings.

In view of Robert's closeness to the memory of Arley's disasters, he concentrated to a large extent on seeking greater safety for the miners, though he was beginning to realise that their own insouciance contributed frequently to underground accidents. He had not long to wait for the next one. In April 1857 there was an explosion down a mine at nearby Hindley (three miles from Ince) that killed nine men and boys outright. It was a minor disaster compared with the horrific death totals at Ince Hall 1853 (58 killed) and 1854 (89 dead), but it was sufficiently worrying in that it confirmed the ongoing vulnerability of the pits in the immediate area, where the explosive nature of the disasters indicated clearly that gassy seams were the chief source of loss of life. In fact the period 1853-1870 has been designated the Era of Frequent Disasters. Robert himself bore witness to or attended the fallout of no fewer than 23 catastrophes while he worked in the Wigan area. His evening vigil as the corpses were carried out of the Hindley mine not only revived his memory of the Argoed disaster, but was the first of many occasions where he lent solace and rescue efforts to accidents which took place within a dozen miles of his home.

The density of mine localisation in Wigan (as many as 108 at one time) intensified the level of suffering that the borough experienced. Staggering numbers of men and boys were crushed, gassed, drowned, burnt or suffocated together with horrendous frequency. Major mine disasters were always national news. People in more sheltered communities gazed aghast at pictures of lugubrious body retrievals, mournful funeral processions, desperate rescue parties (many of whom also perished). *The Illustrated London News* (founded in 1842) pounced upon the subject of pit disasters as a sensational news topic – their striking engravings made the most of a subject which dismally lent itself to the most graphic representation. The industrial scenery of Wigan and nearby Lancashire settlements appeared regularly in the form of original drawings of eye-witness accounts by local artists.

*   *   *

Almost two years to the day after little Jacob's birth, Mary had another child, Mary Elizabeth, who, fortunately, had a more robust mien. Alas, one month after her birth, Jacob died, in February, aged 2 years and one month. This was almost the norm in young families of that time in the area. Robert and Mary were down to two children again. Mary sought solace in her Calvinist beliefs. The following year Robert registered as a member in Rodney Street Baptist Church in Wigan. The family determined to bring up their children within Church life. In the same year – 1860 – another pit explosion killed 13 men and boys in nearby Winstanley. At this time the total number of mines in Lancashire was increasing rapidly. In 1858 there were 380 mines in the county producing eight million tons of coal a year. By 1874

Mid-19th century disaster scene

there were 558 pits producing 16 million tons. This rate of growth prejudiced careful practices in construction and safety precautions. Too much money was being made. To get the whole picture, British coalfields turned out 64 million tons in 1854 and doubled it to 126 million tons in 1873. In Wigan and its districts up to 75 per cent of males worked down the pit.

Robert Lewis was a consistent advocate of seeking close bonds – unity if possible – between different mining communities. Having seen the lack of cohesion or coordination of activity between the pitmen of North Wales and South Lancashire, he constantly looked around for allies within reach. In this regard he made several brief sallies to Cheshire and later on to Staffordshire. In 1858 he had managed to help convene a national conference at Ashton-under-Lyne, where delegates attended from Yorkshire, Cheshire, Staffordshire and even Scotland. At this meeting he made the acquaintance of another labour leader, Alexander MacDonald, a former student of Glasgow

Bringing the dead out of the shafts at Haydock Colliery

University, a fluent speaker with moderate views, who later was instrumental in getting the Mines Regulation Act of 1860 passed. Robert was generally disappointed with the Ashton conference, which served to underline the inadequacy of meaningful cooperation between the Lancashire and Cheshire delegations.

Two years later, Robert and Pickard switched their focus to try to form a strong district association and attempted this with 13 lodges in Wigan, jointly campaigning for a pay increase. Efforts faltered for some time, but when, in an atmosphere of desperation, a meeting was held in the notorious Scholes to resist a pay cut of 10 per cent, a further meeting was proposed and held in Wigan Market Square. At this gathering the miners unanimously rejected the pay cut and Robert and Pickard reported to the masters that everybody was standing firm. A strike was announced; the coal owners immediately capitulated and withdrew the proposed reduction.

It was a significant turning point. A new Union was formed – the Miners' General Sick and Provident Benefit Society – one of Robert Lewis's pet projects. For the rest of his life he remained one of the driving forces behind this organisation which in the following months expanded its membership in Hindley, Aspull, Pemberton and Ashton-in-Makerfield.

The new union soon ran into trouble in its recruitment policies, as it became apparent that, in spite of its popularity, the subscription fees proved too high for poverty-stricken pitmen. All manner of persuasion was employed – perhaps they could manage with less tobacco and beer – but a set-back occurred when the secretary of the Society, James MacDonald (**not** Alexander) admitted he was too poor to pay his subscription. If that was not bad enough, after selling his mining-gear, MacDonald absconded with the union funds, supposedly locked up in a strongbox bolted by three locks. The poor man was subsequently hauled back from his refuge (Glasgow) and the money (£125) was recovered.

Robert and Pickard persevered with the Union and within a year had secured 4,000 memberships from over one hundred lodges. The unfortunate MacDonald, who in his own way had awakened a spark of interest in the Union and its finances, was sentenced to 10 years imprisonment.

*   *   *

We turn back the clock to 1 January 1861, when a significant event occurred in the Lewis family at Rock Farm. On that day was born a vigorous infant, a boy, to Robert and Mary. They stuck tenaciously to the name of their deceased son – Jacob – insistingly honouring the grandfather. This second young Jake, heralding in the New Year, was different from all the Lewises who had preceded him. Robust at birth, he developed great physical strength as he grew, worked 65 years as a record-breaking collier, founded a dynasty of five sons all of whom he educated, and was the first of the Welsh Lewises to live a normal life span. This personal future was of course unknowable in January 1861 – the same year that Russia announced the abolition of slavery (the Americans emancipated their slaves two years later). Slavery down the pits of Britain was to continue for at least another 50 years involving degradation, toil and hardship, equal to that of Russian rural serfs or blacks on the cotton plantations of the American South (and certainly more danger). It is remarkable that Jake Lewis made a career out of it – and not an unsuccessful one.

*   *   *

Later in 1861 there was another explosion at Shevington Colliery in the north part of Wigan, killing 15 miners. Robert redoubled his efforts to address mining hazards and early in 1862 was a co-founder of the Wigan Miners' Provident Benefit Society, a body which concerned itself not so much with wages or compensation, but with the prevention of explosions down the mine, which took a horrible toll of life each year. In some years more than a thousand British pitmen died in accidents at a rate of one death per 350 employed. In 1878 alone, 1400 were killed and many more maimed.

*   *   *

Another son was born to Robert and Mary in 1863. Fortune smiled on them again as the newborn, Tom, was almost a physical match for Jake. In fact in later life Jake and Tom lived and worked side by side as face-work colliers for 63 years. They were inseparable: after marriage they lived in adjoining houses; they walked to the pit together every morning; they silently munched their jackbit together; they hewed and hacked side by side; they walked home in the twilight and smoked their pipes over their evening meal. Their elder brother

"Awaiting bad news", Mesne Lea Colliery, Worsley, 1867

Johnny did not share their closeness as he lived a few miles away; but he too worked 65 years down another pit.

Rock Farm now boasted three healthy sons – the family was rapidly gaining momentum, though still poverty reigned. As yet none of the boys could earn and Mary could not work. Her two brothers continued to contribute to the household budget as Robert's wage alone was insufficient to provide proper nutrition. His day was long – a full shift down the pit and 3 or 4 hours in the evening attending meetings. The house was crowded, but nobody could afford to leave. Mary scrimped and saved where she could. No help was forthcoming from the neighbours – they were half starving too. Jake related to me memories of going to bed night after night hungry, though he never felt utter despair, as hunger was regarded as a normal state of affairs.

*   *   *

The following two years saw three further pit disasters in the Wigan area. In July 1864, six men were killed in a cage collision in the shaft of Blackleyhurst Colliery Ashton-in-Makerfield. In January 1865, five sinkers were killed in a shaft collapse in Douglas Bank Colliery, Wigan, and eight months later another eight miners perished in a winding rope accident in the California Pit in Aspull. Robert Lewis and William Pickard were closely involved in the post mortem investigations of the last two accidents on account of the unusual nature of the tragedies. These are well-described in Jack Nadin's book 'Lancashire Mining Disasters'. I quote excerpts from the Nadin account of the Douglas Bank disaster, which involved the deaths of five sinkers:

Shaft sinking was a very highly skilled and specialised occupation but also extremely dangerous work, usually carried out by teams of men who moved around the country. There were various methods of sinking shafts, such as using steel tubing in water-bearing strata, and later concrete. But the most common method was to line the shaft with a single course of brick. The shaft would be started off, and sunk to a depth of say 12 to 15 feet. Then, specially shaped wooden spars named curbing would be fastened to sidewalls at the bottom of the hole. The brickwork would then be built up to the surface, filling in any voids at the back with small rubble. The process would then be repeated downwards until the coal seam was reached. Shaft sinking could take anything from a year to several years depending on the strata, and final depth of the pit. Dangers in shaft sinking are very evident; those working at the bottom had little protection should anything fall down the pit. Their only option was to throw themselves to the side of the pit, and hope that whatever was falling missed them. The accident at the Douglas Bank Colliery was very different, perhaps unique in Lancashire coal mining history.

The Douglas Bank Colliery was located near to the Pagefield Lock on the Leeds and Liverpool Canal, near Robin Park Stadium, Wigan. Sinking of the colliery started on 19 March 1863. There were to be two shafts at the pit, named the North Shaft and the South Shaft. The South Shaft was 16 feet in diameter, being the downcast and winding shaft. About 300 yards in a northerly direction was the North Shaft, also 16 feet in diameter and used for winding. The headgear at both shafts were built of pitch pine, and consisted of two main legs of 18-inch timber, and two upright legs for the shaft frame of 14-inch timber attached to the main pulley frame.

By January 1865, the shafts had reached and passed the Pemberton Five Feet, the Pemberton Four Feet, and were within yards of the Cannel Mine at a depth of 500 yards. Shortly before nine o'clock on Wednesday 5 January 1865, the shaft sinkers were busy at their work at the bottom of the pit, and had drilled some holes for blasting. They were then raised up the pit, and the shots were fired – everything appeared to be going as planned, and nothing out of the ordinary was envisaged. At ten minutes to nine o'clock, a party of eight men were lowered back into the pit in a hoppet, or large bucket, to remove the rubble caused by the blasting. The winding engineer was surprised to find that the hoppet, for no apparent reason, stopped suddenly in the shaft, a few yards from the bottom of the pit. The engineer was even more surprised, when the winding rope began to sway violently in the shaft; clearly, something was wrong – very wrong. A number of men on the surface

Identifying the dead at Pemberton Colliery

shouted down into the pit, but got no response. Quickly, another party of sinkers was assembled, and a second hoppet was fixed into position, and the men were lowered down the pit. As they neared the bottom, they saw to their sheer horror that the whole of the last secion of shaft walling, 13 yards deep and 16 feet in diameter had collapsed. This had all fallen to the bottom of the pit completely burying the other hoppet along with its human cargo.

The signal was given to stop lowering the men, and all was quiet for a while, then the foreman heard voices from under the tangled mess of bricks — someone at least had survived. A working party was sent down, and load after load of rubble, bricks and rock were raised out of the shaft. After some lengthy work, three of the eight men were rescued alive, the rest discovered some time later dead under the bricks and debris. It appeared that the blasting had dislodged half of the shaft walling and, when the first hoppet was being lowered, the rest came down on top of the men, knocking the hoppet on its side. The five dead men were thrown out of the bucket, the other three happily held on and, amazingly, the hoppet provided cover as the rest of brickwork crashed around them.

Eventually the Douglas Bank Colliery became a productive and profitable pit for the company. It was kept open for a while, officially abandoned on 17 July 1929, after a credible working life of sixty-five years.

The California Pit disaster at Kirkless Hall Colliery in Wigan was also not of the explosive type and again I quote from Nadin's graphic description:

The Kirkless Hall Coal and Iron Company worked a number of mines, coke and ironworks around and across the Leeds and Liverpool Canal from the Kirkless Hall Farm, Wigan. The California Pit had been in existence for a long time, and had an output as great as any of the other pits in the Wigan district. At the time of this accident the pit employed between 300 and 400 colliers and drawers. However, the previous Saturday was "Pay Saturday", consequently the following Monday was "Play Monday" when most of the colliers, having money to spend, would have been worse for drink. It appears that the headaches, or the money, lasted to the following day, Tuesday 12 September 1865, when just 277 lamps were handed out to the men, who descended the pit at the usual time that morning.

With the day's work done, the colliers began ascending the pit shaft, and by a quarter to four that afternoon, about one hundred men had been raised up the 315 yards deep pit. Below ground the men and boys gathered to await their turn to be raised up the pit – eight more colliers and boys were placed in the upper of the two decked cage by the hooker on, and the signal was given to the engineman to raise them up the shaft. The cage rose slowly from the depths of the mine, and the sounds of the waiting colliers far below faded away. The cage slowed down when nearing the pit bank at about 45 yards below the surface. The engineman suddenly noticed the winding rope slip off the conical winding drum, and the subsequent jerk snapped the steel rope, the cage then plunging into the depths of the pit, taking its freight of men and boys with it. Those at the bottom realised what was happening and rushed back, just in time to see the cage crash through the thick balks of timber covering the water sump at the bottom of the shaft. Panic ensued as the men below rushed forward to help, if help was of use, to those in the cage. It was soon realised that they were beyond any aid since the cage was submerged in the dank depths of the dark water, and there was no sign of life. At the surface, a temporary capstan was quickly brought into use and, by five o'clock that day, five men were lowered down the shaft. There was little damage to the shaft itself, the cage was fixed by means of steel guide rods in the shaft, although the last 100 yards or so of these steel rods had followed the cage into the sump, and piled up on top of it. As it was deemed that there was no hope at all of the men and boys having survived the drop, those men still below were raised to the surface, before the recovery of the dead commenced. By twenty-past six, all these waiting men, totalling about one hundred, had been hauled to the top of the mine.

Preparations were then begun to recover the unfortunate victims. The cage was fastened to a strong capstan rope, and raised, creaking and groaning out of the sump hole. The water spewed forth and emptied the death trap. The cage was of course completely wrecked, and those inside were fearfully crushed and mangled. As required and instructed, the men were carefully removed from the crumpled structure, and raised to the surface. Here they were placed on carts to be taken to the Running Horses Inn at Aspull, to await the coroner's inquest. All eight were named as:

James Ramsdale, aged 23, of Hindley, a collier, single
John Dunn, aged 17, of Hindley, a drawer, single
George Ingham, aged 17, of Hindley, a drawer, single
John Holland, aged 20, of Ince, a collier, single
William Bradshaw, aged 18, of Hindley, single
Robert Fletcher, aged just 12 years, of New Springs, a pony driver

Mid-19th century disaster scene

Painting the wagons

Robert Eatock, aged 46, of Hindley, collier, married with six children
Edward Anderton, aged 27, a collier, married with two children

It was never determined how, or indeed why the rope should have slipped off the winding drum, causing this mining disaster. The rope was of steel, and about 3¾ inches in diameter, and had only been on the drum since 13 May that year. It was calculated to be able to have taken the strain of ten or twelve tons, more than of sufficient strength for normal winding operations. When the California Pit of the Kirkless Hall colliery was abandoned in 1898, the events of 20 August 1867, would have been a distant memory for most, save those who lost their loved ones that day.

Robert and William Pickard were aghast at the cruel fate of the incidents' victims. In both cases safety regulations had been followed – it was just that in the world of mining it was impossible to foresee the wide range of accidents that could occur. Between them, in Wales and Lancashire, the two leaders had seen death strike in many guises. Explosions, roof falls and flooding were common, but dangers lurked everywhere. Some men simply fell down open pit shafts, miscalculating where they were in relative darkness, or by slipping near the edge, or in one case by walking in backwards in broad daylight. Bodies that had fallen a hundred (or five hundred) yards were grisly spectacles. Often young boys were among the fallen. In Croppers Hill Colliery a lad of 11 years fell 100 yards down the shaft: he had just ascended and lost his balance. A seven year old boy fell out of an ascending cage as it swayed when nearing the top. Three sinkers fell down a shaft they were walling. At Victoria Colliery in Rainford, a miner was killed when the chain on the hoppet he was riding in broke and sent him plunging 80 yards to his death in the pit-eye. The pit-eye was in itself a dangerous place where many people found themselves crushed by descending cages. In Pewfall Colliery a cage flattened two datallers, who died from severe head injuries while another took a glancing blow that removed the whole of his lower jaw and part of his face.

Waggons were constant hazards. A runaway waggon crushed a seven year old boy at Ashtons Green when the brake failed; drawers might slip on upgrades and wagons could come back on them and run them over. A deaf pitman in Arley was flattened by runaway tubs he could not hear. One man riding on top of a loaded tub in Broadoak Colliery was caught by a low roof and had half his skull taken off. A miner in Blackbrook lost three fingers and fractured his arm as he was hooking on a waggon to another (it was hit by a third). Another woman was hit in the chest by the buffer of a runaway and killed instantly.

There were more singular instances of meeting death in and around the pit. At Laffak Colliery two men were drawn over the pulley at

A mass funeral following a mining disaster

the top of the headgear. One was severely mangled, the other freed himself only by jumping down the pit shaft. In Pewfall a Jigger operating a jig (a pulley wheel in the haulage system) was mangled and killed as he was drawn by the chain against the drum. In Sankey Brook a boy cleaning the machinery connected to the engine got his head caught in it and had it almost severed. In Nutgrove Colliery a stoker fell into the winding gear of the engine, suffering fatal mutilation. In Lea Green a boiler man was scalded to death when the boiler exploded in front of him. Other even more original ways of dying were discovered in and around the pits. Pit-brow lassies were often hit by screens (large mechanical riddles where coal was graded at the surface), one deaf lady was run over by a locomotive near the pithead, one pitman crushed another's skull with a hammer after an underground dispute, another threw gunpowder on the fire at a workmate's house in Skelmersdale and burnt it to the ground. Even death struck among coal-pickers as they plundered the colliery heaps – some being buried by cascading coal and rubble. This apparently did not deter the raiders as the practice continued to flourish!

*   *   *

At the turn of the year, Mary, fertile as ever, became pregnant again. In July another boy was born – he was given his father's name, Robert. Less robust than Jake or Tom, the infant survived only 10 weeks, dying in October. One more tiny coffin for Ince Cemetery. The family could ill afford an extra child, but, as in many dirt-poor areas, one pregnancy came hard on the heels of another.

In 1866 it was Ashton-in-Makerfield's turn for disaster. Ashton, four miles south of Wigan, where Robert would spend the last years of his life, boasted several big collieries. Six men had been killed in a cage collision two years earlier, but accumulation of gas caused two massive explosions in January 1866 (High Brooks, 30 killed) and in May (Garswood Park) when another 16 succumbed. Both collieries had dangerous reputations and each suffered several more explosions in the next two to three years.

The New Year of 1867 ushered in another Robert-and-Mary off-spring – a girl they named Margaret. She was healthy and lived till she was 70.The family now boasted five healthy children – boys John, Jake and Tom – plus two girls Mary Elizabeth and Margaret. These youngsters went on to lead normal lives, dying only in their seventies. Jacob I and Robert had died in infancy as did Charlotte their last child born in 1878. Five out of eight was not a bad average in miners' families in the 19th century. Robert's father had lost five out of eight.

Robert was greatly distressed by a horrific explosion which occurred the following year in nearby Hindley Green Colliery. It was a major disaster – 62 miners were killed including a large number of boys. Robert was familiar with the pit and knew many of the men who perished. The whole area was shocked as Springs Pit (Hindley Green Colliery) was supposed to be a safe mine, well-run with minimal gas emissions emanating from the seam. It was a large pit employing 300 men and boys. The downcast shaft was 320 yards deep and 12 feet in diameter. The workings were well-ventilated.

At 6 o'clock the fireman carried out his preliminary inspection of the pit and gave the all clear. The men descended and had been hewing nearly three hours when a big explosion was heard. As both shafts appeared undamaged, there was only limited concern at first, but the underlooker, near the explosion itself, soon ascertained that a considerable number of miners had met instant death devoured by flames raging through the workings subsequent to the explosion. Rescue teams hastened down the mine only to be met by suffocating afterdamp. This slowed their rescue efforts, but gradually the horrific scene revealed itself. Many men were badly burnt, some almost to a cinder. Others had had the flesh torn from their faces in the explosion. Many of those who survived – brought to the surface gassed, scorched, concussed and maimed – added to the death total as they succumbed over the next two or three days. One woman had four sons down that morning – two died and two survived. One man named Highton left a widow and 10 children, while another left nine. In total 20 women lost husbands and over 50 children their fathers. Poignantly the colliery site was taken over by recreation grounds and descendants of those that died play tennis and other sports 300 yards above where their forefathers perished.

CHAPTER 12

Unrest in North Wales

1869 was a momentous year in the history of mining in Britain. In spite of the reforming efforts of William Pickard, Robert Lewis, Thomas Halliday and Joseph Booth, the further penetration of deeper seams in the districts surrounding Wigan triggered explosion after explosion with increasing frequency: Rainford Colliery 16 January, 8 killed; High Brooks Pit, Ashton-in-Makerfield, 1 April, 37 killed; Queen Pit, Haydock, 21 July, 59 killed; Low Hall, Wigan, 15 November, 27 killed. Minor accidents leading to the hospitalisation of pitmen occurred every day. Uneventful weeks were rare; disasters were becoming the norm.

After 13 years in Wigan, Robert was beginning to think, talk and act like a Wiganer. He still favoured moderation when negotiating with the masters, but continual rejection of his proposals, lack of humanitarian behaviour on the part of the coal owners vis-à-vis injured miners and desolate families, persistent inability to make ends meet, gnawing hunger, daily threat of death – all conspired to inject a streak of cynicism into his natural Welsh bent towards reasonable debate. He saw Wiganers were less afraid of open confrontation than Welshmen. The pitmen spoke a fearsome dialect which not only gave them independence and originality of expression, but had a cutting edge of emotive content – it was a weapon of attack used in facing the masters and in their own internal raging. It is normal for a dialect to reflect the life and mood of the area in which it is spoken. A large number of Lancashire dialect words are strongly derogatory or disparaging. The pits and mills of Wigan, the climate, hardship and poverty bred a dialect with a ring of despair, tinged with desperation and aggression. Jake and Tom wallowed in unadulterated dialect from the age of three or four. Nobody in Rock Farm spoke anything else. Robert's Welsh lilt faded slightly in the unavoidable acquisition of Wigan mining vocabulary – *jackbit, baggin, kench, scuftin', thrutchin', take thee hooks*, as well as indicators of rage or frustration such as *maitherin', yammerin', powfagged, maulin', powse, jiggert, roozer*, etc.

Though 1869 spread catastrophe in Wigan, it was however the year when North Wales took centre stage. The Riot of Mold in June, though it was by no means the first major disturbance in the town, nor in Flintshire as a whole, proved to be a landmark event in British mining history inasmuch as the well-publicised fatalities and injuries (including those to innocent bystanders) caused far-reaching changes in the policing of the country and profound soul-searching regarding the role of the British army in controlling riotous behaviour. Accidental death down the pit, even if due to negligence in safety precautions, was one thing. Shooting of protesting pitmen and their wives by soldiers was another.

Robert was well aware of the decades-old background causes of unrest and violent protests of miners in his part of North Wales. The Industrial Revolution created insatiable demands for high quality coal; the canalisation and road improvements south of the Dee meant that Welsh coal could be transported rapidly to Ireland and half of the British Empire. Workers flooded into Flintshire and Denbigh to provide manpower. Mold's population jumped from around 10,000 in 1851 to 15,000 in 1871. The importation of cheap (almost free) Irish labour in this period meant that native Welshmen had to accept derisory wages and cruel working conditions to enable them to get a job at all. Many of them had been rural workers and now turned to

Welsh workers

eking out a living working down the pit in the winter months, then
scuttling back to the farms for two or three months in summer when
demand for heating coal was lower. For most of them it was a life of
virtual slavery in which they were trapped interminably in order to
avoid starvation for themselves and their large families.

Agitation, vehement protests and sporadic violence were inevitable.
Troops were called into Mold as early as 1826, when miners went
on the rampage, destroying property and threatening colliery managers and overseers. These "middle men" were in the pay of absentee
landlords and shareholders and had little interest in offending
their superiors, thus their sympathy for miners' pleas was minimal.
Constant, automatic rejection of workers' demands led to a 7-week
strike at Treuddyn in 1855, one which Robert had supported strongly
while working his last year out at Leeswood. Many of the strikers
had attended his meetings and their action no doubt hastened his
dismissal shortly after the striking pitmen went back to work.

Though based definitively in Wigan after 1856 both in terms of his daily shift work and reformist activities, Robert visited Mold regularly, usually on Sundays, to see his mother and the faithful Robert Savage, who continued to live in Garden Place. He also remained in close touch with his in-laws the Hughes family, several of whom were active in miners' revolts organised in Mold, Leeswood, Treuddyn, Buckley, Coed Talon and adjoining districts. Robert spoke at length with leading activists, describing the parallel agitation that he and Pickard conducted in Wigan and constantly reiterating his intention to coordinate miners' movements in North Wales and South Lancashire. Symbolically, coordination was a natural phenomenon, since a geological map of North Wales shows that the coalfields run from North Wales out through Chesire into Lancashire. Welshmen and Wiganers were hewing different ends of the same seam of cannel!

Since Robert's departure from Mold, Leeswood Colliery had prospered. The Leeswood seam was proving to be one of the richest in North Wales. The cannel, extracted at a depth of 100 yards, lay below the main coal strata and fetched the best prices on account of its high quality. In the 1860s Leeswood Green was producing some 8,000 tonnes of coal weekly at an average of 15 shillings per tonne. The North Wales coalfield as a whole produced more than 2 million tonnes in 1864.

Fortunes were being made, but the creation of such wealth proved irrelevant to the fate of the miners who toiled to make it possible. Wages remained rock bottom and pitmen had no guarantee that even the current rate would be maintained or indeed if they could work a full week. Things had got worse since Robert Lewis had gone to Lancashire. In 1859 Leeswood, like most collieries in North Wales, had been taken over by the English; gradually Welshmen at managerial or overseer level were replaced by Englishmen who proved to have little sympathy for the plight or aspirations of the local pitmen. Many of the newcomers were from Durham, others from Lancashire. At hewer level, Welsh miners got on fairly well with the 'Lankies', as they were called, but Geordies seem to have been less compatible.

At overseer level, favouritism was usually shown to Englishmen, who were given the most fruitful seams to work on. As far as the actual Welsh landowners were concerned, matters were no better, if not worse. Welsh aristocracy had made their pact with the English Crown and nobility in previous centuries and lived a life of comfort and privilege, sometimes over the border. Their children were educated in private schools, their income, besides that from farming, was now dramatically increased by the discovery of coal under their land. They did not even need to work with it. The colliery owners and investors paid them handsome royalties. Consequently the Welsh working classes could expect no help from their own more fortunate countrymen. The same of course applied to Wigan pitmen. Such was life in Victorian Britain and the Industrial Revolution.

But Robert learned on his visits to Flintshire that things in Leeswood Green, at least, were coming to a head. In 1863 there had been serious disturbances when six local families were evicted by the English manager of the Coed Talon Coal Company and Lancashire people took their places. Welsh fury began to be directed more at overseers and colliery managers rather than at the owners themselves. In 1868 three such managers were marched off to the railway station and forced to buy tickets to distant destinations. As has been mentioned before, it was the Welsh way of ridding themselves of people they could not tolerate. It was a rough procedure, but the victims were rarely harmed physically and there was a certain humour in it. Departing officials were often unable to protest specifically, as the miners taunted them in Welsh as they waited for the train. The miners' wives often attended such packings-off, adding to the overseers' humiliation.

A Durham-born underground manager named John Young was appointed to Leeswood Green Colliery in 1864 and spent the next five years making himself extremely unpopular with the workforce. He did not hesitate to give the best seams in the mine to his favourite workers – all from England – and often Geordies like himself. He set himself up as a disciplinarian and made no bones about disliking

Welsh people in general. Mold pitmen found themselves working in low, unproductive seams and trucking large amounts of shale and waste to the surface (which brought no recompense). When Young was accused of prejudicing Welshmen in this way or failing to give them decent seams to work on, he simply denied it. He scorned the Welsh language in his presence, and when the colliery owners decided to ban the use of Welsh at work, he particularly took it upon himself to enforce the rule.

It was in the midst of this climate of suspicion, mistrust and petty injustice that Young, on the morning of 17 May 1869, placed a notice at the pit-head announcing a cut in miners' wages for the following two weeks. Many of the pitmen had just had their wages reduced by half, due to hitting a fault which let water into the pit. The new cut proved to be the last straw for the pitmen, who argued in vain with Young for the next two days. On 19 May tempers on both sides flared out of control and after prolonged taunting, posturing and pushing, Young was allegedly assaulted by the furious pitmen. This incident, which I shall describe in detail in the second part of this chapter, led to the notorious Mold Riot, the repercussions of which were felt not only by Robert and his fellow countrymen, but by the working classes of the whole nation in their attitude to the powers of the authorities, their licence to keep law and order, their callous verdict on the killings and the one-sided sentencing approved by the magistrates.

*   *   *

There are two versions of the incidents leading up to the actual riot. According to John Young, he was aggressively surrounded by two or three hundred men at the pit-head after he had taken breakfast. They were not all Leeswood men but seemed to represent a cross-section of miners from neighbouring collieries. They hemmed him in and angrily demanded his resignation. When he pointed out that wage cuts were not proposed by him, but was a decision made by the management, out of his control, they brooked no argument, pushing him roughly and finally knocking him to the ground where his clothing was soaked in dirty puddles. The shouting pitmen thwarted his attempts to regain his feet, beating him around his neck. A man called Thomas Jones kicked him in the side and he feared for his life as another man threatened to beat him over the head with a stout piece of wood. When he eventually was allowed up he was held by two men he knew – William Hughes and Edwin Jones – and told he would be packed off at the railway station in the usual Welsh manner. Young asked to be allowed to go home to change his clothes, but his attackers were in no mood to concede anything, so, after being held captive for 45 minutes, he was frog-marched through Leeswood and on to Hope Junction station outside Penyfford. The crowd had now grown to 300 colliers, jubilant at the prospect of Young's departure. The colliers handed him over to two constables, PC McBride and PC Jones of Pontblyddyn police, who escorted him by train to Mold where he made a statement to Superintendent Thomas of the Flintshire Constabulary. The next day Thomas went to Black Diamond Colliery in Coed-Talon and arrested William Hughes (a relative, incidentally, of Robert Lewis's wife Mary) who was taken into custody. A crowd of 300 miners and their wives assembled in front of Mold Police Station in the Hall Fields and demanded Hughes's release. In view of the "ugly attitude" of the crowd, the police decided to bring Hughes out of his cell and release him. He was subsequently carried shoulder high down Wrexham Street and on to Leeswood and the Black Diamond Colliery at Coed-Talon.

Later in the day David Phillips, a 39-year old miner at Cae Blyddyn Colliery, who had earlier been a prize-fighter in Carmarthenshire, talked with Hughes and persuaded him to turn himself in to the police, advocating non-violent pressure to get rid of Young. Hughes concurred and was released on £60 bail to appear at special sessions at Mold Court House on 2 June.

Before discussing the Court proceedings let us take a look at the second version of the 19 May gathering at the pit-head. If one accepts the account given by the miners, the encounter was a confrontation (admittedly an angry one) with Young rather than an assault on him.

Witnesses asserted that he was not wilfully knocked to the ground but that the untrammelled pushing and jostling of the crowd resulted in his falling, as others on the scene did. In such a melee, it was hardly possible to be sure who was in a position to do what. Apparently, Young was not shoved into the empty coal tub, he simply lost his balance and fell into it. As for his allegation that he was kicked in the ribs by a certain Thomas Jones, it was proved that Jones had not been anywhere in the crowd at the time. It seems likely that Young, though certainly being roughed up to some extent, suffered no serious physical harm. When he was examined by Superintendent Thomas an hour after leaving his "attackers", there was no mention or evidence of even minor injuries. His clothes were soaking wet, yes, but no more than those of miners who on occasion might have to work an eight hour shift in flooded mine workings. In view of the privations and injustices suffered by hundreds of pitmen under Young's rule, it would be reasonable to conclude that the overseer got off lightly on the day. It is questionable if he would have been treated so leniently at the hands of pitmen from the Scholes!

CHAPTER 13

The Mold Riot of 1869

It has been estimated that between 500 and 1,000 people assembled outside Mold Court House on 2 June, the day of the trial. The crowd consisted almost entirely of colliers from all the pits in the vicinity. Their wives and children accompanied them; the Court House itself was packed. Such a show of solidarity undoubtedly gave the Welsh mining community a feeling of strength in numbers, a belief in the justice of their cause, and some expectation of a favourable verdict being returned in the face of such unswerving local support for the defendants. They were to be cruelly disappointed.

The eight men who appeared before the magistrates charged with assaulting John Young were Ishmael Jones, William Hughes, Edwin Jones, Robert Davies, John Jones, Richard Taylor, Thomas Jones and John Hughes. The lawyers for the prosecution and defence laid out their cases before seven magistrates: C. S. Trevor-Roper, John Wynne-Eyton, Edward Pemberton, Colonel Willis, Henry Potts, the Revd. Jenkin-Davies and C. Butler-Clough. The fact that four out of the seven had double-barreled names and most of them were either landowners or had mining interests perhaps should have spelled out a warning with regard to a lenient verdict.

John Young, of course, was the principal witness and, as the evidence unfolded, it became obvious that it boiled down to which version of events the magistrates would believe: Young's or that of the accused pitmen. The discrepancies stood out: Young was noted for his disparaging remarks about the Welsh; he asserted he got on well with the men. He was accused by the colliers of allocating fruitful seams to his English favourites ('fancy-men'); this he denied categorically. It was asserted that the English colliers made significantly more money per week on account of this favouritism and ledgers were produced in court proving this; Young denied all knowledge of such accounts. The defence asserted that he had hindered the provision of a suffi-cient number of pit props to keep wages down; he claimed he had no control over the supply. It was asserted that he had verbally assaulted William Hughes' wife for being Irish and had called her a Fenian. He denied this and would not admit that he had said to her, "You will all be eating peelings before long". The injuries Young claimed he had suffered were discounted by the defence on complete lack of evidence of blood or even abrasions. Young told the magistrates that he had been frequently abused in the Welsh language, though admitting that he could not understand Welsh.

The subsequent verdicts issued by the magistrates indicated that they accepted Young's word on every issue. Apart from the unlike-lihood of parts of his testimony, the court failed to establish why warrants had been issued without the proper procedure (previous summonses); they also ignored completely the concrete evidence pre-sented in court with regard to the relatively low earnings of the Welsh pitmen compared to those of the Englishmen working in the same pit.

The magistrates, having heard all the arguments, retired for consul-tation. After what seemed to be a very brief retirement they returned to announce the verdict. Trevor-Roper, the chairman, who allowed himself the liberty of bellowing at the five defendants, announced a finding of guilt on all counts. He went on to inform them of their sentences. His words were related verbatim in a following edition of the 'Wrexham Advertiser'. This was the newspaper's account:

"Ishmael Jones and John Jones: It appears you were the ringleaders, and committed the most severe offence upon Mr. Young, and therefore we have decided that you shall be imprisoned and kept to hard labour for one month. (There were expressions of surprise in court.) With regard to William Hughes and Edwin Jones, we think you were there aiding and abetting, and though it does not appear that you struck Mr. Young, we fine you 10s. each and costs, or one week's imprisonment. Robert Davies, Richard Taylor, Thomas Jones, and John Hughes, you all committed an assault, and you are fined £1 and costs, or 14 days' hard labour. It is very much to be regretted that you behaved yourselves in such a manner. There seems to have been a very strong feeling against Mr. Young, but really after the evidence we have heard, there seems to have been no occasion for it. We hear that he said this and the other, but it has not been shown that he has done so, although still it will be for the consideration of the directors whether they will retain him after such bad feeling has been created. It does not appear that these Englishmen were more favoured and therefore there was no occasion to treat Mr. Young in the way you did treat him. I hope this will be a warning to you never to take the law into your own hands again, because the magistrates have the power of punishing you if you do. The last time you behaved exceedingly roughly, but to-day so far there has been no complaint, and you do not come, as before, armed with sticks, but have brought your wives and children, and therefore we suppose there will be no row. I hope this will be a warning to you, and I recommend you to go home quietly and peaceably."

In view of what happened in the following two hours, Trevor-Roper's final advice is endowed with great significance.

The Court rose at 5 o'clock. It seemed incredible that the proceedings had taken only six hours to reach conclusion. A contested case today might take a week or more and would certainly be brought before a jury. It seems that the magistrates, perhaps influenced by certain parties behind the scenes, were in a hurry to make examples of the revolting miners. Trevor-Roper in particular chose to be selective in his consideration of the evidence and spoke harshly to the defendants in front of a packed courtroom. The newspaper account continues:

As the crowd inside exited from the buildings, on the steps of the hall David Phillips who from the beginning of the disturbances had exerted himself very much with the men, and through whose persuasion the men were induced to come forward without putting the warrants into force, addressed a few words to the men, with the intention of congratulating them on the lenient manner in which the cases had been dealt with. He said they had gained one point and more, but it was true that two of their number were to go to prison. Many in the crowd immediately got exasperated, and said aloud, "They shall not go." Women also went about saying, "We shall not go home without taking the men with us." A large crowd waited outside the hall, many of them adhering to their determination to prevent Ishmael Jones and John Jones being taken to prison.

THE ATTACK

After the event of rescuing the prisoner Hughes on the first hearing of the case a week ago, the authorities had made extensive preparations to meet a similar attempt. The Chief Constable had issued orders that the whole strength of the force should assemble at Mold on this day, and in obedience to those orders the county police, to the number of 39 or 40, were in town at an early hour on Wednesday, Superintendents Thomas, Adams, and Bolton, with all the inspectors, sergeants, and constables in their respective divisions, appeared in their new helmets, and armed with cutlasses.

Up to eleven o'clock the town received a continual influx of colliers, many being accompanied by their wives and children, and with the exception of a few lads the colliers generally appeared without cudgels or sticks, so that a general impression prevailed in the early part of the day that the people were peaceably disposed, and that whatever became of the eight men who surrendered for their trial there was no danger of a repetition of the rescuing business, and of placing all law and order at defiance. When the detachment of fifty men of the 2nd battalion of the 4th Regiment of "the King's Own", under the command of Captain Blake, arrived in the town in full arms with the ten o'clock train from Chester, the public felt an additional assurance that the colliers, though numbering five or six hundred altogether, would not, unarmed as they were, risk an encounter with the military. But in this the public were griev-ously disappointed. It appeared that the colliers had fostered the expectation that all the prisoners would be set at liberty on paying a nominal fine. They would listen to no other arrangement than the release of the prisoners on their own conditions. Numbers crowded on the railway bridge, whilst a large crowd posted themselves in the new road leading to the Free Church, which is an elevation, giving great advantage for an attack upon any persons below in the neighbourhood of the railway station. Several men were noticed walking along the turnpike road to Flint, as if they intended laying in wait lest the prisoners should be taken along that way. But the greater portion were in the neighbourhood of the County Hall and the Railway Station. At a quarter-past seven the prisoners were brought out to be in readiness to proceed by the 7:15 train via Chester. The military marched in front of the prisoners. A crowd closely followed, and as soon as they got through the gates of the County Hall grounds they began to pelt the military and police officers with stones. It so unfortunately happened that all around the place there were abundance of loose stones ready at hand – on the railway bridge, the road leading to the Free Church, as well as the road to the station, which is a somewhat steep incline to the station. *In addition to these there were large heaps of stones that had been got out of a gravel pit near the Victoria Hotel, and were lying ready for carting. Women were seen filling their aprons with stones to supply the men with abundance of ammunition. When the escort reached the gate opening to the platform at the station it had been locked to prevent a rush into the station, and the military were thus forced into a corner from whence they could not stir for several minutes – some said for ten minutes or more – exposed to a complete shower of stones of different sizes, varying in weight from a few ounces to 3½ lbs or 4 lbs, which did frightful injuries to the military and the police. Ultimately the prisoners were got into the station through the telegraph office, the door of which is situated outside the railings and gate, a number of the soldiers pushed in as well. The telegraph office then became the chief object of attack, and all the window-glass was soon cleared away, and the door panels knocked into splinters, the large stones doing great damage to the furniture inside. The prisoners were got away from this place without the observance of the crowd, but they shortly afterwards found out or suspected that they had been placed in the train, which next became the object of attack, the glasses of several windows being smashed, and the passengers inside becoming alarmed, several rushing out and crossing through the wharf, and went to their homes through the fields. As a private of the detachment named Tipper was entering the telegraph office, he received a severe blow with a stone on the side of his face; he was considered in such a dangerous state that it was advisable to despatch him by the train to Chester. Captain Blake was knocked down and severely injured; and Sergeant Wood and Private John Carrol received serious cuts on their heads, the latter's nose also having been badly wounded. Altogether two officers and twenty privates of the detachment were roughly treated and badly wounded.*

Almost all the police officers were more or less injured, about twelve of them being severely cut on their heads or faces. The

THE RIOT AT MOLD, FLINTSHIRE: ATTACK ON THE SOLDIERS AT THE RAILWAY STATION.—SEE PAGE 691.

The Mold Riot

Chief Constable had his wrist damaged and he was also lamed. Superintendent Thomas was severely cut on the head, so also was Inspector Hughes. Dr. Williams was most energetic in bandaging and dressing the wounds of the military and the police officers, upwards of twenty passing through his hands in a short time. He was assisted by other medical officers.

P.C. McBride, of Pontblyddyn, alone turned round and faced the crowd, returning upon some of them the stones which they had so mercilessly hurled at the officers.

The prisoners themselves did their best to help the crowd, and kicked most violently the officers who were conducting them; but it was thought they also must have received some blows with stones.

The Chief Constable was most attentive to the men under his charge, supplying them with water and stimulants.

FIRING ON THE RIOTERS

After the greatest forbearance had been exercised by the soldiers and the police, the crowd pressing on them most unbearably, and a rattle of stones on their shakos and helmets, and against the wall increasing, the word of command was given to the military to fire. At first they fired over the heads of the mob; but this evidently only had the effect of exasperating the rioters, for they still continued to stone the soldiers and the police. The troops again fired – this time into the thick of the mob – and with terrible effect; for the result of the second discharge was that several persons were killed or wounded. The first to succumb to a shot was a young man named Edward Bellis, aged 21, from Coed Talon, who was within a few yards of the military, some persons who alleged they had seen him, stated that he was both throwing stones and using a huge stick. He received a shot in the left side, the bullet penetrating below the heart to the abdomen. He was refused admission at the Druid Inn, and then conveyed to the Queen's Arms Inn, Pontblyddyn, where he was at once admitted, and attended to by Dr. Platt, but the wound was of so severe a nature that he died at one o'clock on Thursday morning.

Another man – Robert Hanaby, of Moss, near Wrexham – stood behind the iron hurdles in front of the Free Church. He had been noticed by several parties to be very active in throwing stones, when a shot caught him on the cheek bone, entering the head and causing the brain to protrude. He fell at once, and was presently carried to the yard of the Victoria Hotel, where he died in a few minutes. It is said that this man was picked out by one of the military, who observing his activity popped him off.

Bullet holes

The third shot which proved fatal was one received by an innocent young woman (Margaret Younghusband), who had nothing whatever to do with the disturbance of the colliers. She came over to Mold a few days ago with the intention of engaging as a servant in a respectable family in High-street. On this unfortunate day she with others had been employed to clean the Presbyterian chapel in New-street. That work had just been completed and she was paid for her labour, when she ran with the crowd down towards the station. Standing on the hill below the turnpike gate, the poor unfortunate girl was shot in the groin, and conveyed to Dr. Williams's surgery in High-street, where in a very short space of time she expired. She was an orphan girl, but had several friends and relatives in Mold, and the corpse was taken to an aunt of hers living in Garden Place to prepare for the funeral arrangements.

A woman named Elizabeth Jones, wife of Isaac Jones, of the Black Diamond, Coed Talon, received a shot at the back which came

out at the chest. It has been stated by some who said they saw
her getting stones for the men to throw at the soldiers and police.
Her husband was with her in town, both taking an interest in the
proceedings that were going on. She was attended by Drs. Hughes,
Trubshaw, and others, who were of opinion at first that she could
not live twelve hours. Mr. Charles Keam, manager of the Mold
Union Iron Foundry, was standing near the railings of the Free
Church, looking on, when a shot caught him on the right arm, the
ball going right through. Not very strong hopes of his recovery are
being entertained.

These were the serious injuries that were brought to light, but it
is currently reported that minor cases also took place. The marks
of the lead in the parapet wall of the railway bridge and the front
of the County Hall are numerous. One ball went right through
the front door – of thick, solid oak – passing out through a side
window.

When the mob found that the soldiers had actually fired upon
them, they fled in all directions. The Rev. Jenkin Davies and Mr.
Clough, two county magistrates, were present with the soldiers and
police during all the row, and we believe the responsibility of firing
will not rest on the individual shoulders of officers or privates.
The mob who attempted to rescue the prisoners was estimated at
between 1,000 and 2,000 persons.

After the firing the prisoners were safely sent off by the train, and
were not taken to Flint, as was at first intended, because it was
feared that an attempt would be made to rescue them. The pris-
oners were consequently taken to the castle at Chester, where they
were lodged for the night, and were removed back to Flint county
gaol in the course of Thursday. The troops who had been in contact
with the rioters returned to Chester on Wednesday night by a train
at ten o'clock, and another detachment, consisting of 108 men,

under the command of Major Paton, relieved them in their duty at Mold. The soldiers who returned to Chester bore very decided marks of the seriousness of the conflict, and their appearance indicated how severely they had suffered at the hands of the rioters. Some of the men were covered with blood, and others had received wounds about the head and face, and altogether they presented a very battered aspect. The military in Mold are at present quartered in the Market Hall, and the headquarters of the officers are at the Black Lion Hotel. After the attack on the troops it was feared that the rioters might endeavour to get possession of the rifles known to be stored in the volunteer armoury, and to prevent this, the permanent staff of the Flintshire militia, stationed in the militia barracks at Mold, were placed on duty to resist any attack which might be made upon the barracks.

The disturbances were not, however, renewed during the night. The town presented its wonted quiet appearance. The only unusual occurrence to be observed was the number of persons congregated at corners discussing the recent disturbance, and the presence in the streets of policemen with their heads bandaged, and troops doing duty at the Market Hall.

THE INQUEST

On 4 June, an inquiry touching the death of Edward Bellis, Robert Hanaby, and Margaret Younghusband was opened at the Boar's Head Inn, at 3 p.m. before Peter Parry Esq. After being sworn, they proceeded to view the bodies, and were conveyed in vehicles to Pontblyddyn to view that of Bellis. When the jury re-assembled after viewing the bodies, the Coroner suggested the propriety of adjourning the court in order that evidence might be procured.

One or two of the jurors remarked that the case might be disposed of that night, as they themselves knew of the occurrence, and others

Railway station, Mold, where the 2 June 1869 riot took place

expressed an opinion that delaying it would keep the town in a state of commotion and excitement, and that if they adjourned for a week they would then have no more evidence at their command that they had at the present time. Those who had been spectators of the conflict considered that the military had been most severely treated and had shown great patience before they fired upon the people.

Referring to some dissatisfaction in the town as to the soldiers firing before the Riot Act was read, the Coroner said that if life was in danger and people used threats, the military had a right to turn and kill, and they could not tell when they fired upon persons whether they were rioters or not. If by accident, therefore, they killed one who was not a rioter, they could not be held responsible. He believed there was evidence to show that women, as well as men, threw stones. There were only a few police there and there were many hundreds of rioters, and with the number there were there the police could not be expected to defend themselves. The

police had not been able to defend themselves, and the military had
to interfere. They forbore a great deal, and that spoke very much
in their favour but when they were attacked and their own lives
were in danger, they had a perfect right to turn and shoot and kill.
It would be for the jury to listen to the soldiers and police wishing
to give evidence.

The inquest was adjourned until the following day, 5 June, when a
verdict was returned that Bellis, Hanaby and Younghusband had
met their deaths by justifiable homicide. The jury placed on record
their "sympathy with the military and police under Captain Blake
and Mr P. Browne respectively, who forbore for so long a time from
doing what they eventually did". The trial of 10 rioters who had been
arrested after the riot broke up was fixed for 6 August.

The inquest failed to investigate a series of issues, left many questions unanswered and ignored gathering evidence that cast a doubt
on the validity and credibility of key people involved. The numerous
loose ends would be addressed with some intensity in the following
days and weeks by Robert Lewis who was expedited hastily to Mold
when news of the riot reached Wigan.

Robert Lewis had worked his day shift on 2 June, had had his tea
with Mary, Jake and Tom and was going through some union reports
around nine o'clock when Jack Johnson burst through the front door
with an urgent message from William Pickard who had been tel-
egraphed the news of the riot and shootings. Halliday was rushing
to Wigan from Bolton where he had been talking to coalowners.
Pickard had arranged for both of them to meet up with Robert at the
Royal Hotel.

When Robert arrived at the hotel, the bar and adjoining rooms
were heaving with shouting pitmen, some of them straight from
work with clogs and black faces, gesticulating angrily, spilling beer
over tables and the wooden floors. The three miners' leaders huddled
together in a corner as far as they could get from the hubbub. Halliday
was in a vicious mood, Pickard was moved but matter of fact, Robert

was nervous and on edge, anxious to go to Mold as soon as possible to ascertain what had happened to his kith and kin. The other two concurred, but advised him to attend a briefing of union members they would convene the next day to agree on a strategy for his visit. Pickard assured Robert that his relatives were not among the five victims of the shooting. He expected further information that night. Halliday also wanted to hasten to Mold, but Pickard, knowing the temper of his colleague, insisted that Robert was the man to send – a native of Mold who would be able, through his many connections with pitmen at several levels, and with his fluent Welsh, to assess the situation more accurately than anybody else at their disposal.

The next day twenty-odd members of the district union assembled in the Boys Well Fields in Wigan, joined by half a dozen Mold miners who had arrived by train. They confirmed that the members of the Lewis family in Garden Place were all safe and sound, though William Hughes had been re-arrested after the riot. The town was full of military and further arrests were expected. The Welshmen also considered it likely that another outbreak of violence would occur over the next few days and urged the meeting to send Robert Lewis to the area as soon as possible to calm his former workmates down and avoid further bloodshed. He would also be needed to convene miners' meetings, as he so often had done more than a decade earlier. His name was highly respected in North Wales and his reputation for forthrightness tempered by moderation would benefit the volatile situation.

Robert needed no urging and travelled by train to his native town the next day.

Wigan Pier

Pub at the Pier

Thirsty miner?

Overlooking Wigan Pier

By the River Douglas

Life was hard

The Scholes today

Scholes Monument

Wigan Town Hall, formerly Mining College

Ince Cemetery

Mold Riot

Welsh workers

Bullet holes at the Court

The Cape

A legend of his time

Wigan Mill

CHAPTER 14

Agitation in Mold

He found Mold in a state of great agitation. Soldiers were everywhere in the streets and cafés, small groups of Welsh people gathered at street corners, muttering in Welsh, avoiding eye contact with the soldiers, who themselves looked uncomfortable. Robert tried to elicit impressions from them – most remained tight-lipped and turned away. Fine weather and summer clothes contrasted with the grim atmosphere and the general sense of shock. The inquest, scheduled for the following day, was in everyone's thoughts.

Robert went over to Leeswood, where most of the men had failed to work their shifts. He sought out familiar faces, asked about what they had seen. The majority of them had been in the rioting crowd. They were seething in anger for the most part, but spoke guardedly, even when speaking Welsh, aware of the presence of the military, nervous overseers and strangers. Robert decided to wait a couple of days before holding a formal meeting, though he put everyone on notice that this would take place in nearby Brymbo the following week. He spent several hours with various members of the Hughes family, incensed at the re-arrest of William Hughes. His mother and Robert Savage were both on edge. She, particularly, referred to her warning of fifteen years earlier, albeit opposing implacably the conduct of the authorities. Robert himself considered he bore no blame for the tragedy, as he had always counselled moderation, but felt furious at the catastrophic outcome and killings.

Everybody wanted to see him. He reluctantly agreed to have a meeting after the summary result of the inquest on the following day. The sharp verdict of "justifiable homicide" stung the miners to the quick. Robert could not turn pitmen away – they were justifiably enraged – but he gathered two dozen of them in nearby Northop, where they held a stormy meeting away from the eyes and ears of the soldiers and Mold authorities. Proposals for revenge were many, but none made sense to Robert. Physical attacks on anyone in or out of uniform would result in immediate arrest and incarceration. Several wanted to go on a rampage and wreck mining property and public buildings (as had occurred in Wigan some years earlier). Robert pointed out that any such wreckage would lead to loss of the only jobs available in the area, not to mention years in jail. After the tragedy of the shooting – of Welsh people on Welsh soil – the frustration of not being able to retaliate was unbearable to the more emotional pitmen. Robert was dismayed at their predicament, but he told them coldly that the only hope of getting even was not through pointless violence, but to organize themselves in such a way that the authorities would be obliged to take them seriously. For Robert, that meant numbers – not only having a determined common purpose in North Wales, but uniting themselves quickly with the tens of thousands of frustrated pitmen in nearby Lancashire, not yet shot at but fearless in their attitude to the authorities and thirsting for revenge for the endless humiliation they suffered daily. When some of the Welsh said they could not trust the English, Robert almost laughed aloud.

"I am one of you, a Welshman, but now I'm a Wiganer too, and I can tell you that these southern Lankies will fight our battles for us once the battles lines are drawn. They hate the English Establishment more than we do and will never cave in once they start something. I wear two hats – I'm one of their leaders as well as one of yours. But we have to unionize quickly and not just talk about it. There are thousands more in Cheshire and Staffordshire I have talked to. In fact they worry that the Welsh will not support them enough. I think our aggression in Mold has woken them up to see what part the Welsh can play, but we've got to keep our heads down for a few months until we're ready to move."

The following week, Robert spoke to a miners' assembly in Brymbo, where he gave an outstanding speech on behalf of the wronged Mold men in detention. It had not been easy to organize the meeting since he had not been able to find anyone able or willing to print his bills. However his reputation as a speaker was such that 900 miners turned up to hear him. His tone was fiery, indignant, logical, occasionally sarcastic:

Relations between owners, overseers and pitmen at Leeswood had been deteriorating for a decade – strikes and demonstrations had been frequent events. Had it not occurred to the authorities that some-thing ought to be done to improve the situation? It was well known that miners and their families were starving – where could one look for humanity? Workers' requests were often reasonable; why were they always refused out of hand? Where was the so-called English 'fair play'? Was it not obvious to all that owners and workers were all in the same boat and that if production failed, through strikes or simply malnutrition, would not the masters be the biggest losers? Was it necessary to bring in unpopular Geordies to manage honest Welsh workers and if one of them proved so ruthless and insulting and blatantly anti-Welsh, would it not have been sensible to replace him? Did the English think that there was no end to Welsh patience? When the matter eventually came to court, even before the violence, had it been the sensible policy to take the Geordie's word before that of Welsh witnesses on every occasion? Aren't magistrates supposed to be fair and impartial? Mister Young got wet when he slipped to the ground. Did he know how pitmen got soaked from wet seams and had to squelch on for eight hours through the shift? There must be some sympathy for our soldiers and police who suffered abrasions caused by stones; how many abrasions did a pitman get in a month's work through falling lumps of coal, maybe ten or twenty pounds at a time, if not the whole roof?

Robert, not wishing to sound too flippant, turned to legalities: why had seven miners been arrested on warrant so speedily, on 25 May? The local police knew the normal procedure was to issue summonses for them to appear before the court and only issue warrants for their arrest if they should not appear. The police knew all the men personally. Did they think the miners were going to 'take their hooks', quit their jobs and flee to the mountains? Robert himself had had many encounters with the local police and had found them often sympathetic to the miners' cause. Why had they acted differently, and so hastily, this time? Who was behind it? But that was a minor matter compared with the shooting. Was it not the law of England that if 'rioters' were to assemble, the Riot Act had to be read out to them and time given for them to disperse, before the police could take whatever action they chose to split them up? Had the Riot Act been read on 2 June? We all know it was not. How could the soldiers be authorised to shoot if it had not been read? Who authorised the shooting? We all know that such authority must be given by a magistrate. We are told that a certain Mr Clough gave the order. Was he really a magistrate? As far as I can gather, he was a passenger on the train! What a convenient coincidence! Has anyone seen him since? Apparently he was scared to death himself when he gave the order. It seems that Captain Blake insisted that the Riot Act should be read before he would allow his men to fire, but in the end our precious Mr Clough got round it. I would have expected any shooting, however unjustified, would be properly aimed at offenders. Yet, it seems that it was indiscriminate in several cases. At least two innocent bystanders were shot and others wounded. Four people died! I hope Mr Clough slept well that night.

I would also like to have a few words with the coroner, Peter Parry of Mold. The jury at the inquest consisted of 15 local tradesmen who are hardly likely to have been happy with the course of events. But from all accounts that have reached me, Her Majesty's Coroner told the jury that in no circumstances could the army be held responsible for people's deaths. How much evidence was submitted to the inquest? Not a scrap I am told. None of the victims were represented at the inquest. Out of 300 colliers at Leeswood Green only four were allowed to give evidence – it was all in favour of the defendants. Why was the evidence, presented in court, relating to the discrepancy in pay between the Welsh and the English, completely ignored? Magistrates are supposed to be neutral. Yet one of them, Thomas Wynne-Eyton, actually owned the Leeswood Green Colliery, where all the trouble started! John Young, our loveable Geordie, was Wynne-Eyton's representative at the pit. The Coroner took it upon himself to convince the jury that the miners were the only villains of the piece. How did he express it? *"It is in the working classes interest especially that laws should be supported, for it is to the law they must look for the protection of their rights and protection of their property. If the law was once invaded, there would be an end to the rights and privileges of the working classes of this country – one of the great privileges which we as **Englishmen** enjoy".* And Welshmen?

CHAPTER 15

The Amalgamated Association of Miners

Robert returned to Wigan after the Brymbo meeting and reported limited success to Pickard and Halliday. The 900 men who had attended his meeting had been unanimous in their support for progress towards unionisation, but he considered their organisational abilities weak and in Flintshire at least he felt they lacked credible leadership. There was too much hot-headedness and absence of planning, even a spirit of despair in the face of the brutality of the shooting and the implacability of the authorities. He realised, albeit modestly, that nobody had taken his place as an inspirational pacesetter on his departure in 1856. He felt the tug of his native town – should he return to Mold and attempt coordination from there? Mary would not have objected – she never felt even half a Wiganer – but Robert actually did. Johnny, Jake and Tom were real dialect-wielding Wiganers by now, but the most important reason mitigating against a return to Wales was the influence he had acquired on a much bigger stage. He and Pickard were making names for themselves as effective miners' leaders and organisers. Wigan was coal HQ and the nerve centre of colliers' revolt: The Mold riot, though occurring in a little-known location, had sparked off a rebellion among pitmen in the big towns in Lancashire, Yorkshire and the North East. Though Robert's account of his meeting in Brymbo had been modest, it had been attended by all the local pits and the final resolution was "to consider the desirability of forming a colliers' union in the neighbourhood."

Robert's next and immediate step was to organise a conference of Lancashire miners in the Mechanics' Institute in Manchester, which attracted 100 delegates. Alexander MacDonald and William Pickard were President and Vice-chairman respectively. Robert headed the largest delegation from Wigan, with 54 delegates. All the others were from Lancashire: Oldham, St. Helens, Farnworth, Kearsley, Poynton, Worsley and Ashton-under-Lyne. A decision declared that "efforts should be made throughout the country to build an amalgamated association" and Will Pickard and Robert Lewis were deputed to establish it. They were instructed to "undertake a thorough organisa-tion of the miners of the country: its necessity and use."

Robert wasted no time in setting about this. His aim was to estab-lish a comprehensive union, which would be named the Amalgamated Association of Miners (AAM). Leaving Wigan for the moment in Pickard's hands, he chaired a series of meetings in the next two months in every part of the North Wales coalfield. His activity culminated in a huge gathering on Wrexham Racecourse in mid-September 1869 attended by 3,000 vociferous miners. Robert spoke for over two hours at the meeting, partly in Welsh for the Mold miners present. A Leeswood collier (Leeswood had established a lodge) spoke out that the union would make it possible for them to liberate the slaves at home, as had recently happened in America. The masters were exhibiting no little nervousness at the frequency of gatherings voicing discontent and tried to infiltrate the meetings as best they could by sending spies. At the Wrexham rally, Robert noticed a stranger in the crowd going from man to man giving some kind of information. After his keynote speech, Robert came down off the platform and fol-lowed the man around to see what he was up to. It turned out he was a Durham colliery owner and was trying to recruit pitmen to replace ones he had recently fired in Durham. Robert confronted the man and asked him if he wished to leave quietly or otherwise. After some

discussion the Durham man backed off and made an undignified exit. It was discovered later that in two hours he had been able to find three recruits and these were not miners.

Robert sensed that Welsh pitmen were emerging from the bitter despair immediately following the Mold Riot. He returned to organize an even bigger rally in Wrexham six months later when the numbers (over 5,000) gave some indication of the dramatic rate of progress of the AAM. Tom Halliday and Will Pickard went to support him. Robert was gratified to see that 1,000 of the miners were from Mold. With his new designation of 'national agitator' he felt he had come a long way from his lone soliloquies near the Leeswood pit-head. Since the Riot, all the chapels and schools had offered him their premises for his meetings. Women frequently paid calls on his mother at Garden Place, praising her son and his campaign. She, often fearful of further reprisals, as was her wont, largely kept her own counsel, but made cups of tea for all callers.

The early days of the AAM were not without problems and setbacks. The Miners' Association of Great Britain, quite separate, had been formed in Wakefield in 1842. It lasted seven years. Another attempt at forming a national union took place in Leeds in 1863 – Pickard and Tom Halliday were Vice-president and Treasurer. This union was christened the MNA (Miners National Association). It was in fact a miscellaneous collection of mining unions and eventually became dominated by the Durham and Yorkshire collieries. These rich county organisations were reluctant to join Robert's AAM, they had no wish to squander their hard-earned wealth with an aggressive centralized union which intended to back smaller members everywhere, and perhaps lose money doing it. MNA levies were small in comparison with AAM's. The AAM supported the Welsh strike of 1871 with many levies from Lancashire pitmen and elsewhere. The MNA's loose federal structure would not work in Wales or Staffordshire, where previous failures had proved they could not stand alone. Robert pushed for a tight, centralized structure which ensured sustained overall support, in essence, unity.

The difficulties of surveying

There were deep rifts within the AAM. Bolton miners were suspicious of Wigan pitmen who worked longer hours, received less pay, but produced more than they did. When the campaign in South Wales was strongly supported, Lancashire miners resented their precious levies paid for it. The executive's prerogative to determine strike policy was frequently challenged by the rank-and-file. The big test came when the AAM lent its full support to the South Wales strike of 1871. Coal prices were rising nationwide and the Steam Coal Collieries Association, which fought the strike, failed to keep in employment a large number of Stafford miners who were for a while blacklegs. The strike lasted 12 weeks and resulted in a favourable settlement for the AAM. The demand for a wage cut had been defeated: a two and a half per cent increase was conceded.

After the South Wales strike, the AAM was treated with greater respect in other areas. Robert, always the champion of moderation,

Dissenter Ground, Ince Cemetery

expressed, on behalf of the AAM, willingness to settle disputes by arbitration. This he had long wanted in Mold, but it had always been rejected out of hand. The answer had been dismissal. A Liberal politician A.J. Mandella, wrote a letter to the Mayor of Wigan suggesting an arbitration court be set up in the area. The idea was discussed at length and eventually dropped, as Halliday and others did not see the need for interlopers, but in the following months arbitration was employed to settle various disputes.

The next push of the union was for Lancashire's benefit, as they had backed the South Welshmen stoutly with their levies (not always too happily). A general meeting was held at Hindley, near Wigan, in April 1871 to discuss wage increases. Robert and Pickard felt the moment was ripe to give Halliday his head. The latter, in his capacity of President of the AAM, conducted the struggle personally and succeeded in achieving unprecedented increases in pitmen's pay. From August 1871 to April 1873 wages rose at an average of 60 per cent. Wigan miners suddenly found themselves the highest paid colliers in

Moss Colliery disaster memorial

the Amalgamated Association. Workers flocked to the union in grati-
tude. Membership topped the 100,000 mark in 1874. It is reported
that pitmen started wearing clean shirts and coloured ties, gorgeous
'belchers' round their throats, polished their boots on Saturday nights
(even in the Scholes), smoked big cigars and even tried drinking cham-
pagne. It does not appear that Robert Lewis shared in this affluence
(his mother would have deplored it) but the family's diet improved
dramatically. It was a pleasant period in Robert's life as he saw he had
achieved some betterment of his co-workers' lives in Lancashire –
something he had not been able to do in North Wales.

*   *   *

Encouraged by their victory over the Steam Coal Association, Robert
Lewis and William Pickard held rally after rally in different parts of
Lancashire and Cheshire. Such was Robert's popularity as a speaker
that he was given another hat to wear – that of miners' agent for the
St. Helens and Haydock District of the AAM, a post which had seen
little continuity. Pickard, Davison and Rhymer had all tried to run
this district but it had been noted for poor discipline, hot-headed
pitmen and volatile behaviour. Robert, through his oratorical ability
and unfailing firmness, brought a great degree of stability to the area.
His usefulness as a well-liked ambassador for the miners' cause led
to his setting up the first branch of the AAM in North Staffordshire
after addressing workers in Burslem, Hanley and Longton. In June
1871, he took charge of a huge miners' meeting at the White Lion Inn,
Church Street, St. Helens, where he made a decisive speech ensuring
overall support for the 9,000 striking miners in South Wales, who
had had a five per cent reduction in wages. Many Lancashire pitmen
were lukewarm about aiding the distant Welshmen. Robert empha-
sized the broader view.

"If this drop in wages in South Wales is maintained, South Welsh
coal will be produced cheaper and the masters there will be able
to undersell the colliery lords in Lancashire. In the long term the
Lancashire masters will have to match Welsh coal prices, and you

can guess how they will do that – by reducing **your** wages by five per cent or more! It is essential that St. Helens miners, as well as all the others in the AAM, show solidarity with our Welsh brethren. We have already sent them £1,000 for relief, but I can tell you that is nowhere near enough. We have to increase this sum greatly and right now!"

It is reported that he won over his audience completely. His conscientious bearing, selflessness and humanity were apparent for all to see. He had himself worked a full shift that day. They knew that he was paid little or nothing by the AAM. Simplicity was part of his charm. One of his favourite pulpits was an old cart in the middle of Boys Well Fields in the Scholes. In 1872 he addressed an unprecedentally huge assembly from this cart, where the AAM demonstrated their strength. Delegates were sent by 100 lodges and seven bands celebrated their presence. Robert was able to report a promising development in the St. Helens district, where AAM membership had grown from 500 to 1,500 in three months and concluded terms of six to seven shillings a day for an eight hour shift. Two weeks later he roused a huge crowd in Walsall.

From 1872 to 1873 Robert was a busy man – too busy, in fact. Besides racing between his four 'constituencies' – Wigan, St. Helens, Staffordshire and North Wales, he attended conferences in Bolton, Burnley, Bristol, Manchester and South Wales with increasing frequency. He was also the Treasurer and driving force of the Wigan Miners Provident Benefit Society, an organisation which faced increasing problems and responsibilities in view of the incessant pit disasters and the resultant claims of victims. Robert and Pickard rushed from tragedy to tragedy at this time. An explosion at Queen Pit, Haydock killed 59 miners. A fire at Low Hall, Wigan killed 27. A sickening disaster occurred at Moss Colliery, Ince in September 1871, where 70 men and boys perished. A memorial column was erected in Ince Cemetery, a few hundred yards from Rock Farm. The constant travelling, speaking and scheming, on top of a daily shift, began to take a toll on Robert's health. Considering the poor diet he had been encumbered with for many years, he had shown unbelievable stamina and fortitude. He was a bundle of energy and gave his all to whatever task he undertook. His sons John and Jake were contributing to the family budget in 1870 (Jake started down the pit at the age of nine), so that the family ate meat two or three times a week. That probably kept Robert going for a few years more, but the continual strain and worry that his work entailed, as well as the responsibility of bringing up five young children, had an effect on his heart. Miraculously he did not take time off work, but Jake recounted in later life that his father complained frequently of pains in his chest before going to bed.

Paradoxically, his wife Mary succumbed well before him. She was physically strong and had not suffered frequent illness – only colds, rheumatism and chronic backache – but child-bearing, sixteen hour days and cheap food along with the constant struggle to uphold reasonable sanitary conditions, had worn her out. She never stopped carrying out her household duties and put meals on the table two or three times a day as men and children wandered in and out according to their schedules. By 1871 when she was 35 years old, her sons John and Jake were already coming home in black faces and pit clothes, adding to the daily washing and scrubbing. During her last two years she was fading fast with angina. She gave birth to their last child, Charlotte, on 14 January 1873. Charlotte lived only two years. Mary survived the birth by only two months and died (officially of myocarditis) in March 1873, two months short of her 38th birthday. She was buried in Dissenter ground in Ince Cemetery, sharing a communal grave with William Meadows, eight others of the Meadows family, and a Thomas Walsh, miner.

CHAPTER 16

The Decline of the AAM

Pressure of work led to Robert resigning his membership of the Rodney Street Baptist Church in 1871 but in the same year an Ebenezer Methodist Church was established a few hundred yards from his home between Ince Cemetery and Rock Farm. Like many miners, he had been a Methodist or a Baptist all his life. It came as a surprise to those who knew him, particularly to his own children, when he re-married four months after Mary's death at St. Oswald's Roman Catholic Church in Ashton-in-Makerfield. His new wife, Alice Rose, a twice-widowed provisions dealer at Sims Lane End (between Garswood and Ashton) was indeed a practising Catholic. She was 38, Robert was 42. In the mining communities at the end of the 19th century, quick re-marriage was not unusual. Widowers with young children needed a wife to look after them, widows needed a new husband to provide an income, however sparse. As Alice was in the grocery business, food for the Lewis children became more accessible, though Jake told that he and Tom were not fond of their stepmother – a strong-willed woman who married a fourth time after Robert's death.

There was, however, plenty of life left in Robert Lewis, who spent the whole of 1873 campaigning in St. Helens, Stafford, Bristol,

Farnworth, Burnley and all the Wigan districts. In November he had
the greatest fright of his life when he learnt of an explosion in the
Bare Bones Colliery in Gidlow, Wigan. It was the pit where Jake,
now 12 years old, was employed. The accident was reported to have
killed seven face-workers, some of whom Robert knew. He hastened
to the pit-head and was relieved to find Jake morosely sipping tea
surrounded by half a dozen pit lads. Jake, who had been thrutching
a hundred yards from the explosion, had been thrown off balance
by the blast, but was fortunately unharmed. As it turned out, he
enjoyed good fortune throughout his 65 years of mining, often seeing
injury and death at close quarters, but never suffering a major injury.
Though Robert had lost many friends in pit disasters, his own three
sons survived a combined 190 years of underground activity, breaking
nothing except their noses.

*   *   *

1874 was a difficult year for Robert and the Amalgamated Association
of Miners. The early seventies had seen dramatic rises in the price of
coal. This benefited the coalowners but displeased industrialists and
domestic consumers. The average price of coal rose from 18 shillings
a ton in 1870 to 32 shillings in 1873. The problem, both for factory
owners and the man in the street, was that there was no alternative
form of fuel to turn to. Wood had become scarce, oil and electricity
were not around. The industrial dependence on steam meant that the
consumption of coal increased rapidly in tandem with the growth of
industry.

Another factor emerged: as time goes by, coal is more difficult
to mine. As seams close to the surface are mined first, shafts have
to be sunk deeper and deeper to get at bigger seams. In 1874 the
shaft at Rose Bridge, near Wigan, reached over 800 yards; others
in Lancashire were deeper. The Wigan Observer estimated that the
sinking of a single shaft could cost between £40,000 and £100,000.
Coal cutters and improved haulage equipment, high speed cages and
other forms of machinery added to the owner's cost. Coal mining was

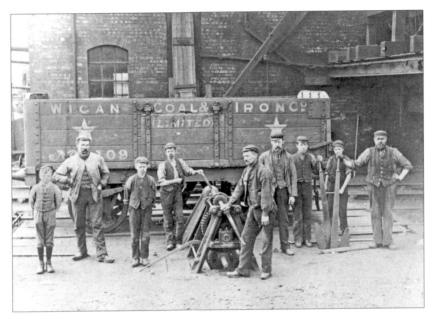

Group photo

becoming a very capital intensive industry. (One can draw a parallel with the 21st century oil industry, where wells penetrate deeper into the sea-bed in places such as Northern Norway, the Arctic and the Gulf of Mexico, thus driving up the price of oil, the modern substitute for coal).

Miners who had benefited from the wage boom of the early seventies soon showed a tendency towards absenteeism. They were able to maintain their modest standards by spending less time underground and working less. As coal prices rose, output declined. This worsened relations between coalowners and colliers. Standards of productivity varied; one owner of two mines, one in Durham and one in South Wales, declared that output per man was almost double in the north-east.

As profits plunged in the down cycle after 1874, the militancy of the AAM began to work against the interests of the colliers. Robert Lewis had been pleased with the union's growing strength and the raising of miners' living standards that he had struggled for for so long, but he felt, along with Pickard, that things were sometimes going too far. Coalowners were being called upon to invest huge sums in order to achieve output targets, but profits were melting away. The AAM, instead of co-operating fully with masters who were trying to keep the industry alive, were showing increased militancy bordering on arrogance. The union insisted on the custom of taking tubs from miners in strict rotation, which meant that fast workers (such as Jake and Tom) had to stand by idle while slower workers struggled to keep up. Two-shift working was proposed and accepted by the MNA in the prosperous Durham area, but was rejected out of hand by Halliday on behalf of Lancashire and South Wales colliers.

AAM decisions were taken by a few leaders at 75 Piccadilly, Manchester, which was in effect too narrow a base. Talented miners' leaders in other areas were not sufficiently consulted. Consequently they often disagreed with union policy and smaller unions started to pursue their own course. The historical separatism of Lancashire mining districts began to rear its head at the expense of AAM central control. The Wigan districts saw Tyldesley leave the union first, followed by Skelmersdale in 1874 and Standish and Oldham in 1875.

Splits such as these repeated themselves in many parts of the organisation. The national leadership found itself unable to impose too tough a discipline on its affiliated bodies for fear of them leaving to join the rival National Association, with its smaller levies. This happened with Oldham, as well as with Cumberland and parts of North Lancashire. The downswing of the trade cycle drained the coffers of the AAM. As money ran out, the normally militant Halliday advised acceptance of swingeing wage cuts proposed by the increasingly harassed owners. He went too far in compromising the men's position and made himself a subject of attack from both sides. He arranged an open air meeting to argue the case for acceptance. The meeting dragged on until dark, ending in a supposed vote, which Halliday, in a letter to the secretary of the coalowners' association, said signalled acceptance of a 10 per cent reduction. Robert Lewis considered that

Halliday had manipulated the open air meeting and he led the Wigan and St. Helens miners to pass a vote of censure on Halliday. In a reversal of his and Halliday's wonted positions on negotiating, Robert declared that Halliday had no authority to sign a paper accepting the proposed cuts. "The men would rather fight and be beaten and have a 20 per cent reduction than accept a 10 per cent one dishonestly."

Halliday was now out of favour, William Pickard stood momentarily aside from the discussion. On 15 October, Robert Lewis denounced Halliday's motives at a large gathering which initiated a miners' strike in the town of St. Helens. This followed instructions by the St. Helens union to Robert to secede from the AAM. A week later, on 23 October, it was rumoured that men at the Haydock collieries of Richard Evans and Co. had accepted a 15% reduction of wages. Robert Lewis then organized a parade of 1,500 miners from St. Helens to Haydock in order to meet at Blackbrook School Rooms to elect a deputation to confront the masters. This attracted a large number of rowdy onlookers and as the procession continued, with Robert at its head, stones began to be thrown and it was feared that something similar to the Mold Riot might develop. Robert Lewis halted the parade and remonstrated with the crowd and (according to a report in the Liverpool Mercury) urged them to remain calm or go home. He was nevertheless arrested by the police, along with James Tatlock, an official of the St. Helens district. Both were charged with "causing unlawful and riotous assembly". Arrest was nothing new for Robert who, mindful of the times he had been detained in Mold, assumed that he would be acquitted. They were committed to the Kirkdale Quarter Sessions and released on £50 bail. On the 7th of November at the Sessions, Robert produced a host of witnesses who bore testimony to the fact that he had repeatedly cautioned the crowd. He pointed out that it was initially a peaceful parade. He also submitted that the real reason for his and Tatlock's arrest was to put down the strike. Both men were acquitted, being found not guilty by the jury after one hour's debate.

The St. Helens men, however, lost the issue with a reduction of 15% by the St. Helens masters, following the collapse of the Amalgamated Association of Miners and its merger with the newly-created Miners National Union (MNU). Robert Lewis continued as Agent for the St. Helens district.

In January 1875 the South Wales coalowners, who had never liked Halliday, took advantage of his current unpopularity and firmly decided to impose a wage cut. Soon 50,000 miners in S. Wales were idle. Halliday strived to achieve a settlement, but the owners stated flatly that they would not negotiate with him. They added that they would only talk to the more moderate union, the National Association. Robert Lewis, whose influence was strongest in Lancashire and the North, was unable to help. Halliday saw the AAM's looming bankruptcy. When the National Association made approaches for unity of the two organisations, the AAM leaders grabbed the chance. A joint meeting was held at Leeds Town Hall where it was agreed that a new union, named the Miners National Union (MNU) would be formed and run on federal lines. The system of centralized control – Robert Lewis's creation – was abandoned.

CHAPTER 17

Robert's Last Days

Paradoxically, this decision strengthened Robert's hand, since the sizeable local unions of Wigan and St. Helens, which he controlled, were now able to pass resolutions which favoured local requirements. Nevertheless he never abandoned his vision of greater unity among miners. In 1876 he participated in the formation of the Lancashire and Cheshire Miners' unions and spoke out in favour of all Lodges becoming part of the new Union. The following year it became apparent that the North Staffordshire miners were in need of more cohesive guidance and Robert was invited to assist in a complete reorganisation of the movement there, frequently visiting North Stafford, Burslem and Longton. In early 1880 he took his attempt at unity a step further by being active in a newly-created Federation of Miners Associations. It was widely reported that he was considering accepting an offer to be the North Staffordshire agent, but his ties to Wigan and St. Helens made this impractical.

His last major speech was held at the White Horse Inn, Little Lever, Nr. Bolton on 24 July 1880. The purpose of the meeting, which had a large attendance of colliers, was to restore unity amongst the men with a view of obtaining an advance of wages before October.

Robert began with a lengthy report on the present position of miners generally:

"In times when we have been properly organized, our efforts have been crowned with success. A good example is the AAM victory in the S. Wales strike of 9,000 men in 1871. A wage reduction was being forced upon us, but by dint of stout resistance and supporting each other with hard-earned levies we triumphed and obtained an increase in wages. Though we have followed our separate ways to some extent since 1875, we have finally witnessed another step forward with the passing in Parliament of the Employers Liability Bill most recently. This is in effect a direct threat to the coalowner-dominated Lancashire and Cheshire Permanent Relief Society. Masters' control of the funds has meant that we have had to take what we were offered. This national scheme now gives us the chance of more miner control. Now I warn you that this new Bill will be of no use to you unless you are properly organized. Suppose a miner is killed or maimed and his case requires being taken into a court of law, where will the money come from to pursue the case successfully and obtain the family's rights and the compensation due to him? Remember that the Weighing Clause, which was granted to us in 1872, turned out to be nothing more than a blank paper when we tried to get our entitlements.

The miners in Yorkshire, West Cumberland, Northumberland, Durham, Staffordshire and South Wales have achieved advances in wages and secured the sliding scale on account of being more united than we are. As a result of disunion in the Wigan districts – unfortunately a historical tendency – we have fared worse than our co-workers in other areas. I cannot urge you enough – unite and stick together – otherwise you will always be taken advantage of. If we look what has happened in Pennsylvania, a deal has been struck between masters and men to restrict output, so as to ensure a uniform price for coal and a proper rate of wages for the miner. The same is now being done in France and Germany, which will certainly produce beneficial results. We have had some success in Staffordshire in getting a sliding scale, but, as we have improved the organisation there, they have the will to move on and have declared their willingness to pay for the hire of the Mechanics' Hall in Manchester, so that the betterment of the miners' lot may be discussed at a conference of delegates from all parts of the country. This conference is due to be held on 10 August. Please awake from your slumbers here in Little Lever and attend this meeting!

Since 1862 I have taken an active part in the miners' societies and for my part I have seen nothing to keep them from demanding their rights but their present and continual state of disorganisation. Why don't you look at the positions of other trades? Engineers, masons, bricklayers – they all enjoy more rights and privileges than you. That is because they are organized. Remember that in 1869 we achieved unity through the formation of the AAM, but the economic situation in the late seventies conspired to wreck our union. We must however make efforts to unite again. How long are colliers going to remain so vulnerable? What kind of game do the powers that be play with us? We have been trifled with at every point. First the Game Laws had to be attended to, then the Salmon Fisheries Bill. The fish in the sea, the fowl in the air, the cattle in the field must all be looked after, but the poor working miner may be burned till he can't be recognized, have his back broken or blown to atoms and nothing will be given to him or his dependants. One man or woman cannot afford to go to a court of law to obtain justice. Miners are thwarted at every turn. I am a simple miner who wishes more than anything to see an improvement of our life's condition. I have worked down the mine for 41 years and I believe I have served my apprenticeship."

Robert concluded his remarks amidst thunderous applause. He remained humble but resolute to the last. A few weeks later, after proceeding to St. Helens to address a rally, he collapsed and died on 15 November 1880. The Staffordshire Daily Sentinel the following day commented on his demise:

> *It is with regret that we announce the death of Mr. Robert Lewis, agent in this district for the Amalgamated Association of Miners, which took place very suddenly near St. Helens on Wednesday last. The Deceased had been ailing for some time, but, though ill in health, had manfully stuck to his post. So late as Tuesday he held meetings in Silverdale and he then proceeded to St. Helens in connection with the work in the neighbourhood to-day. His loss will be much felt amongst miners generally, and his place not easily filled. He was ever an ardent and temperate advocate of the rights of the working man. In January 1870 he was the first person to found branches of the Amalgamated Association in this district.*

*   *   *

Robert's personal estate was just under £40. Administration was granted to his widow, Alice Lewis of Sims Lane End. He was buried at Birchley R.C. Church, Billinge, Nr. Wigan on 18 November 1880.

CHAPTER 18

Coal's Paradox

When I look back on my great-grandfather's life – its honest endeavour, its earnestness, its struggle against cruel odds, its persevering humanity, its recurring tragedies, its sad brevity – I am constrained to look for meaning, for relevance, for grains of comfort, for a warm thread of continuity reaching me through his son Jake and then my father.

It is easy to be negative about coal and its impact on the course of human history. It can be seen, in contrast with marble or granite, as a dirty, black rock whose smoke blocks out sunshine, the lack of which afflicts people living in mining districts with rickets, bowed legs, flat feet, sunken cheeks, pallid skin, curved spines and a host of other physical deficiencies, especially among children.

Methods of extracting coal and their attendant hardships are described in full in Chapter 3 of this book. The advantages gained by Britain in developing the first industrial revolution in the world were savagely offset by the resultant problems of becoming the world's most urbanised society. Rapid urbanisation brought with it nasty air, inadequate sanitation, a spate of diseases such as cholera, diphtheria, scurvy and scarlet fever, destruction of nature, unhealthy and dangerous structures and environments , (both underground and on the surface), the creation of an oppressed and increasingly isolated under-class, the brutalisation of their children and a quick deterioration of family life. Teenagers leaving home to marry young and have a large number of legitimate or illegitimate offspring had no recourse other than to send them to the mine or mill at eight or nine years of age, to miss out on a childhood they themselves had never known.

There seems to be no glamour attached to coal, unlike oil, with its links to jet travel and billionaires. Coal is instinctively associ-ated with the poor – a poverty-stricken malnourished yet frequently drunken and reputedly aggressive segment of society that saw their income base and privileges shrink alarmingly at the same rate that an increasingly solvent middle-class widened its place in society and an elite class acquired undreamt of riches. This was veritable slave labour in 19th century Britain, managed by a so-called Establishment whose galloping profits encouraged them to degrade and humiliate the men who produced them, in order to widen their own margins. The striking injustice of the era needs no further elaboration. Yet how could the extraction of coal under such circumstances be tolerated for any length of time? Had coal, like gold, cast an invidious spell on those who sought to acquire and own it? Was the black mineral in effect a kind of curse on a large section of the British people, a period of tragedy involving horrible disasters and loss of life, a second Black Death visiting the poor once more, a blemish on mankind's record of development, a backward step from the healthy life and clear air that our island's bountiful nature permits, an unfortunate discovery better ignored or wiped from our memory? Was Robert's life in all its drudgery (shared by thousands of pitmen) merely an irrelevance in history, a study in futility, a life better not to have been lived? His achievements were legion and selfless, his moments of happiness scanty and fleeting. His life's rewards were those of a miner from birth to death. Did miners know happiness? A deep, rich vein of coal runs through British history – how many lives were irrevocably blighted by its discovery and extraction?

TIED IN A TRUCK AND HAULED UP 900 FEET: A PIT PONY BROUGHT
TO THE SURFACE AT PEMBERTON COLLIERY, NEAR WIGAN.

There is another side to the story of coal. In her fascinating book "Coal – a human history", Barbara Freese portrays it as not only a boon to humanity, but as a glorious commodity and – wait for it – a romantic one. The extraction of coal, involving untold protracted suffering for thousands of families, brutalized whole communities. It also gave us civilization as we know it. The benefits of electricity and the comforts it facilitated barely reached 19th century Lancashire, but Robert initially and subsequently his sons witnessed the meteoric rise of industrial Britain, the creation of the biggest empire that the world has ever known, the global dominance of Britain's navy, the mushrooming production of iron, steel and cotton – all fuelled by Britain's black mineral. Historical hegemonies previously exercised by Egypt, Rome, China, France and Spain paled into 19th century insignificance before the rise of a small rural kingdom which, through its carboniferous riches, dominated world commerce and politics for over a hundred years.

Coal is friendly, in its way. First judged as dirty, on closer inspection it is the cleanest of rocks. Wipe the face of a solid piece of cannel or anthracite and it comes up smooth, shining, pristine. Coal brought with it heat, light, strength, power – the wealth of civilization. Its absence brought cold, darkness, weakness, poverty – the tedium of the pre-industrial age. It was difficult to mine, but once on the surface it could transport itself: half an ounce of coal in an engine could move two tons of it a mile! What a boon, too, for the railways. And for making a fire – the use of which is one of the distinguishing features of our species.

Miners and their families like to be near coal, they have an affinity with it. Freese goes to great lengths to show *how* coal is intertwined with human destiny in more ways than we might imagine. It has an ancient pedigree, as she explains: coal is the highly concentrated vestige of extinct life forms that once dominated the planet. Preceding mammals and dinosaurs by millions of years, these life forms (originally giant trees) were themselves a critical link in the chain of environmental changes that made the emergence of advanced life possible. While earth's land masses remained utterly barren for four and a half billion years, the story of life unfolded in sheltering seas where vast coal seams lay. When waters became shallow in the carboniferous period 300 million years ago, the exposed lushness drew energy from the sun – plants became peat, then coal. Amphibious life crawled out of the oceans and evolved on land, while coal sank below it. Eventually the land life-forms evolved into creatures capable of digging it up and using it to accelerate civilisation's progress. This wonderful cycle of events led to Barbara Freese's concept of the romance of coal.

Robert Lewis had only a rudimentary notion of the birth of coal, but he, like Jake and other miners of his time and later, was a living part of that cycle. Coal shapes miners' lives; it also shapes their characters. Physically they are bound up with it almost every waking moment. They boil their morning tea over a coal fire, they dress in old pit clothes, they tread blackened soil on their way to the pit, passing blackened buildings under a black sky. Their jackbit carried in an iron tin tastes vaguely of coal, they breathe coal dust as they eat. They hew black stuff all day and return with black faces and bodies to soak in an iron tub. On winter evenings they gather with their families round a coal fire. They are not fazed by any of this, nor by the labour. The work ethic is ingrained in miners – a generational inheritance. Pitmen are permitted to get drunk, steal coal and swear like troopers, but they may not be lazy. Each one strives to avoid this stigma. I have noticed this ethic in their descendants – even those who do not work in mining.

In contrast to his lowly occupation, a miner, especially a second or third generation one, is characterized chiefly by pride. He is proud of his working skills, his strength and his stamina. Allied to these, he has huge reserves of courage, bravery and capacity for self-sacrifice. Besides facing mortal danger daily, he is fearless when called upon to rescue trapped colleagues, risking his life unhesitatingly when another's life may be saved. Forty-four rescuers were killed in one attempt alone. Miners working together are invariably close-knit when facing risk. Their communal spirit and camaraderie are unfailing – their loyalty to bereaved families assured. They have their own moral code: coal-picking is seen almost as a right to compensate for their derisory wage; they will mutilate a dead colleague to secure compensation for his widow. They hate fiercely their enemies – heartless corporate coalowners, yet can show great loyalty to owners of small pits with whom they may have two generations of shared experiences.

Another source of miners' pride is consciousness of their potential political power. At its peak, mining encompassed one million workers. They and their families comprised 10 per cent of the entire population of the country. A strike was a devastating weapon, yet pitmen and their leaders have often used it sparingly. Though one per cent of the population of Britain owned two-thirds of the country's wealth and 88 per cent owned nothing, the miners (in the second category) had a certain proprietary sense where the pits were concerned. The landowner owned the land, the machinery belonged to the mining company, but miners felt the *underground* was theirs. They spent most of their lives in this deep subterranean world, they knew its every nook and cranny, it was their working environment, their haven, a second home. They jauntily sauntered along tunnels and lanes where most people feared to tread. The face-worker, who penetrated the maze deepest, was conscious of his status: the aristocrat of manual labour. He showed contempt for danger and towards the masters who exploited him, but his attitude to the mine was ambivalent. His was a hard world, but had he access to a better one? Men such as Robert Lewis were well aware that they and the owners were in the same boat. In the era in which they lived, the hardest fate was lengthy or permanent unemployment. For this reason miners not only continued to work for near-starvation wages, but they accepted reductions when a pit was threatened with bankruptcy or closure, for it was a nostalgic part of their heritage. Miners' feelings about the mine have been described as a complex cocktail of fear, awe, guilt, sympathy and longing. Mining was creative and destructive at the same time: pitmen were caught up in the omnipresent mantle of tension. They feared disaster, but they could not wait to enter their high-speed cage and start their shift. The youngsters followed their fathers and exulted in their new black faces. They played football in clogs.

There is a whole mystique about miners and pits. Life in Mold and Wigan was cruel, bitter and perilous, but pitmen for generation after generation felt lured down the mine. You heard people say "Keep your sons out of the pit, for once you are in you can never get out" and "We knew as kids that life in the mine was hard but we also knew it would claim us". And claim most of them it did. Miners had large families, bigger than they could afford to feed, but each son they sent down the pit distanced them a little more from starvation. Even the daughters were claimed, on the pit-brow. Robert Lewis, self-educated, often expressed his desire to keep his three sons in school, but at the age of nine they all went down. After a few years, hardly any showed strong inclination to leave. Many could not envisage pursuing another career – life was exhausting, but in a way the underground camaraderie diminished a desire to change environment. Above ground too, their communal spirit flourished. In Ashton-in-Makerfield in Joe Gormley's time there were 39 pubs and 20 clubs. Miners and their wives and teenage children occupied them nightly. When pits were closed in large numbers in the 1970s, mining communities fought hard to keep them open. When closure was imminent, pitmen would parade energetically in defiance with two or three bands playing and dozens of flags flying. It was as if miners, conscious that a vein of coal ran deeper through British industrial history than in any other country (Britain produced four-fifths of the world's coal in the 1830s), strove to maintain their place in the modern world with their precious fossil created in the distant past.

In 1835, not long after he had published his classic analysis of American society, French philosopher Alexis de Tocqueville visited Lancashire and touched on the ambivalent attitude and situation of miners when he wrote, "From this foul drain the greatest stream of human industry flows out to fertilize the whole world. From this filthy sewer pure gold flows. Here humanity attains its most complete development and its most brutish; here civilisation works its miracles, and civilized man is turned back almost into a savage".

My great-grandfather lived at a momentous time in British history. A foggy island off the west coast of Europe became, over a period of 75 years, the epicentre of a massive upheaval in world commerce and power. The industrial revolution facilitated the spread of Britain's manufactures, railways and ships world wide, due almost entirely to the exploitation of her coalfields. Robert Lewis was in the middle of it all. Though of humble origin, he played his part in bettering the fate of miners of his time and in ensuing decades. Their world was to be recognized in more ways than one. The disasters that distressed Robert so frequently, revealed the stoicism of pitmen and their families and their communal strength in adversity. The tragedies brought the best out of them, they were nobler and more unselfish than they themselves had thought. The way many survivors behaved in difficult circumstances sent an important message to society. Relatives of victims showed courage in trying to set up little businesses to make ends meet. When their pathetic plans proved non-viable, miners rallied round them to help.

CHAPTER 19

Robert's Legacy

Robert Lewis's early death, occurring when he was at the peak of his oratorical powers and at a time when his rigorous campaigning was beginning to bear fruit in terms of consolidating the miners' unions, was both a personal tragedy and a setback for the movement. Fortunately Robert left behind him more than one legacy. His inspiration to the miners was one; the entry of his three sons into the arena was another. On Robert's death, his eldest son John was 25 years old, had been down the pit 15 years and was a vigorous face-worker. Jake was 19 years old, had been on the face since the age of 17 and if John was vigorous, Jake was prolific. Tom, now 17, had also started on the face and was already known for his strength and power. It was mentioned earlier that the three brothers eventually broke all production records in the Wigan districts. Their aggregated 190 years down the pit meant that Robert had founded a dynasty within the industry. His family could not of course become rich, given the limitations of the period and the nature of the industry, but they were no longer poor, as events were to show.

Jake was the centrepiece of this transformation. All three brothers had significant physical strength, good health and all avoided any serious accident throughout their long careers, but Jake not only turned out more tubs than anybody else – and for a longer period – but he demonstrated a mental fortitude which gained him respect (ultimately fame) in the mining community. He was not only active down the mine, for on the surface he quickly produced five healthy sons by the time he was 34. The first indication of Jake's strength of mind was his pronouncement, when still in his late twenties, that none of his sons would be allowed to go down the pit. This interdiction, coming from a man who was a full-time miner (and who carried on face-working himself for almost **another fifty years**), was nothing less than remarkable. Most miners in the 1890s were resigned to seeing their sons follow them down the pit (at that time it was expected, almost automatic and not in fact unpopular), but Jake's ban was total, final and effective. None of his boys went down the pit, though all of them were connected with mining indirectly, either through railways or, in one case, politics. They were permitted to go down once or twice – to have a look – but that was it. As all of them turned out to be rather intelligent, they had too much sense to contradict their father, whose temper, when he was crossed, was known to be savage.

It is interesting to speculate what Robert Lewis would have thought of Jake's interdiction. It was a rather anomalous scene: Jake and brother Tom tramped daily homewards, black-faced after the morning shift, to be greeted with five white-collar youths, coming home about the same time, to share evening supper. Perhaps Robert would have been disappointed that not even one grandson had followed his profession; on the other hand, it is likely that he would have congratulated his son Jake on his unalterable principle and his ability to back it financially. Jake never left the pit, it was his only source of income, yet he was never short of money. Neither were Tom or John for that matter, though some of their sons went down the pit.

For a Wigan pitman in the 1880s, Jake was astonishingly well-organised and self-confident to boot. There were reasons for this. Though the second surviving son, he was his father's favourite. The first boy named Jacob had died; Robert was determined that his

Jake Lewis

own father's name should live on and Jake the second did it proud. Robert relied on Jake's strength to hold the struggling family together. Though apparently taciturn, Jake had a strong sense of humour and in later life he became a great story-teller. He did not inherit Robert's oratorical powers, but as an adult he showed great aptitude for articulacy. Although he went down the pit at nine (he was nearly ten), he actually got two years more schooling than his brothers. He put them to good use. Robert was a poor writer; Jake learnt to read and write well (his handwriting was neat and clear) and for some reason he developed a love of reading. He did not have time to read much, but he read when he could. The local teachers were competent and Jake had drummed into him basic history, geography, religious instruction, music, woodwork and painting. He excelled at none of these, but wrote good essays for the English teachers. The instruction he received was essential to his independent character. He was never known to spell a word wrongly, or to make an error of addition, subtraction, multiplication or division. He never tried to pronounce or write a word with which he was unfamiliar and he never made a fool of himself before better-read people. Most surprising of all, he had somehow sensed the vital importance of learning *per se* and in later years compelled his sons to submit to years of study to which he himself would have given the widest of berths.

Robert Lewis's Celtic eloquence surpassed by far Jake's knack for articulacy, but as very often happens, it resurfaced after skipping a generation. Jake's eldest son, appropriately named Robert, went into local politics as a miner's agent, became a local preacher as well as a J.P. and in 1930 was elected Mayor of Wigan. Jake, his wife Jane and the other four sons – Jack, Sam, Dick and Tom – occupied the front row of the Town Hall at the investiture, all the men wearing suits, white collars, ties and poker faces. Robert Lewis (the second) went on to be Alderman Lewis, Wigan's Chancellor of the Exchequer, for the next 30 years, when he was given the Freedom of the Borough.

Jake's other four sons had successful careers, three as railway administrators and the fourth, Dick, (ultimately) as an accountant. Only Robert (the mayor) showed oratorical ability, but in the next generation one of Jake's grandsons became a professonial linguist and international lecturer, travelled to 125 countries and was knighted for his achievements in the intercultural field. The wheel had turned full circle for the family of the desperately impecunious Welsh pitman from Mold. The Lewises are very much a Lancashire family now, though half a dozen retired to Wales in locations such as Pwllheli, Prestatyn and Abersoch, where they took with them their Wigan pitmen's accents.

Jake's modest writing ability and clarity of thought led him in his sixties to pen a factual description of his first day down the pit in 1870 – a year important in European history on account of the outbreak of the Franco-Prussian War and the emergence of Bismarck as the Strong Man of the continent. The Wigan area was less affected by these events as by a dreadful series of pit disasters which occurred during 1869. Two explosions at the Queen's Pit had killed 83 men;

The knocker-up

37 more had died at Highbrook's Colliery; 26 perished at Low Hall, Platt Bridge and 11 others at three local pits.

Jake, who knew nothing of the War and had never heard of Bismarck, turned nine in 1870 and went down the pit. He had been looking forward to it for some time. In those days it was the normal thing for boys from poor families to start working from the age of 10 or 11 and if you were big for your age or sturdy enough, then nine would do.

The following account of Jake's début in the mine is based on his notes of the experience. It is worth relating this description in detail, since few people today can comprehend the difficult conditions and physical hardship that confronted the miners of Mold and Wigan in the 1870s and indeed until the First World War. Jake describes the same hazards and dangers that his father Robert had faced. Robert had railed against the inhuman nature of the toil and dastardly surroundings. He made it his life's endeavour to better the miner's lot. Jake, on the other hand, though aware of the horrid injustices, accepted the life as it was and made the best of it. In a sense they both made equal

Thrutching

Hewer and drawer

sacrifices: one in his selfless campaigning, the other taking it on the chin but protecting his children. These are Jake's impressions:

Finally the day arrived when Jake was due for his first morning shift. He and Tom went to bed at nine o'clock on the Sunday night in preparation and they had not seemed to sleep long before they heard a metallic rattle on the window panes. They woke up in consternation and Tom, near to the window, opened it and stuck out a sleepy head. Below him in the street he saw

Cedric Cutts, the knocker-up. In his right hand he held the long stick with the leaded end with which he tapped on the miners' windows to wake them up in time for shifts. He was nobody's friend and he knew it. The only thing he liked about his job was that he always won. They might curse, shout or sneer all they liked. But they always got up. He hated getting up himself.

"Where's Jake?" shouted Cutts

Jake poked out a distrustful head. Cedric addressed him:

"It's half past four and mighty draughty."

"But I thought we only started at six."

"Aye, but that's on the coalface, me lad, and thar not theer yet. Edgar said he'll pick thee up i'ten minutes and take thee."

Edgar Ferris was a miner living two doors away. Jake nodded.

"Aw reet, I'll be theer."

Jake scampered quietly downstairs and grabbed his working clothes off the rocking chair. Vest, pit-drawers, patched trousers, woollen stockings, clogs and jacket with the elbow out.

Jake was trying to be matter-of-fact. He gulped down the glass of water his mother had left on the table and stuffed his bacon sandwiches into his tommy-tin. Licking a greasy finger, he realised how hungry he was. He had had his supper too early. He took out one of the sandwiches and wolfed it down. It was January and, when Jake opened the door, a biting wind blew round his bare feet. His teeth chattered but he stuck it out on the doorstep until Edgar clattered and clanked along a few minutes later.

It was half an hour's walk to the pit-head in Gidlow (a district of Wigan) and Edgar took the opportunity of enlightening Jake a little about the work which awaited him.

"Thi fust day today, Jake?"

"Ah."

"Hoggs says as they are starting thee off as a lasher-on. Tha'll be aw reet, tha'll be wi'me and me drawer on this shift, we'll keep an eye on thee."

Jake knew that Hoggs was some sort of under-manager, but he did not know what a lasher-on was. He decided to find out a little more.

"What does a lasher-on do?"

"Well, tha helps t'drawer to get tubs up to t'shunt and then tha gets 'em on to the main line. Then tha lashes 'em on – tha couples 'em up. When t'pony comes and tha has 'em all coupled up, tha goes with the thrutchers and does a bit o' thrutchin thisell. When yo get 'em up to t'pit-eye, the runners-in will take 'em off yo, then tha takes th'empty tubs back when they've finished with 'em. Dost follow me?"

Jake shook his head.

"Never mind, tha'll see what I mean when we get started."

And that was how it was. First they got into the cage with three other miners. Jake noticed how white their faces were at the beginning of the shift; they seemed to be ailing. He remembered that he had not washed. Not much point in it anyway. His stomach gripped him as the cage descended at speed, but soon they seemed to slow down and stop and then start to climb again. He wondered what they were going up again for. Perhaps they had forgotten to take somebody. After a while the cage came to a halt and everybody got out. The air was warm and blankety and Jake realised that they were down after all. He could have sworn that they had been about to emerge at the top. He looked about him and noticed that there were rails leading right up to the shaft. Edgar told him that this place was the pit-eye. Two black-faced men who nodded a greeting to the new arrivals were the runners-in. Their job was to put full tubs of coal into the cage for winding to the surface. Jake's group left the runners-in behind them and passed through a huge brattice door into a stuffy chamber about

10 feet square. Inside there waited a door-minder who carefully put the first brattice door to before opening a second one at the other end of the chamber and letting them out. Jake felt the hot air waft into him. He gathered that the chamber had something to do ventilation. Now they were on the main line and, swinging their lamps, the miners tramped off down the long tunnel.

It was half an hour's walk to the coal face. Jake walked behind Edgar down the middle of the rails, peering from side to side in the dim, flickering light. Here there was plenty of height and width, the roof being supported by numerous sturdy props and closely-packed black dirt on the sides. The slope flattened out for a few hundred yards and then dipped more steeply than before. They crunched onwards for what seemed an age, until the main tunnel finally came to an end and the single track of rail split into several tracks, which disappeared through narrow openings in the walls in different directions.

There were a number of empty tubs on some of these lines and Edgar told Jake that they would soon be filling them. The place where the converging tracks joined the main one was the shunt and here most of the miners took off their coats and hung them up with their tommy-tins on nails in nearby props. Edgar signalled to one of the other men – his drawer – and, bending a little, told Jake to follow them down one of the side tunnels. Jake obediently pushed his tub after them, as yet with no need to bend, but seeing very little. They went on for five minutes or so, the roof gradually getting lower, until even Jake had to stoop and the tub would hardly pass. The two full-grown men were now bent double and a few moments later they went down on their hands and knees and began to crawl. Jake saw that Edgar held his right arm with the lamp stretched out stiffly in front of him, dragging himself along on his left elbow. The drawer shouted back to Jake to leave his tub where it was, practically jammed against the roof in any case, and follow them so he would be able to see what was happening in front. Jake abandoned his tub, squeezing around the side of it so he could follow the drawer, who was fast disappearing with the light. Dirt from the packed wall dislodged and trickled down Jake's neck as he squeezed through and by the time he had done 10 yards on his hands and knees he felt every inch a miner. He had left his lamp back at the shunt and he could see very little apart from the clogs and posterior of the drawer. It was a queer experience burrowing along like that in the dark and he was surprised how soon he became tired.

Suddenly there was a slight widening and he saw Edgar's lamp find the black glint of coal. Jake was used to seeing coal nearly every day, but for some reason he was impressed by the sight of it now. This coal had something different about it. It looked confident and at home. It had not been shovelled around yet. Jake would have been content to sit down beside it and examine it a short while in the lamp-light. Perhaps stroke some of the shiny parts. Edgar, however, had different ideas. Near the face lay a wicked-looking pick and a heavy shovel. Edgar took the pick himself and gave the shovel to the drawer who backed away to give him working room. Edgar hooked his lamp into the dirt on one side and wriggled around until he could let fly at the coal. The drawer informed Jake that they had only 22 inches to work in and it was one of the lowest roofs they had seen for some months. Edgar could not even swing from his knees, but was compelled to lie full length on his stomach and swing his pick laterally. Hampered in this manner, an unaccustomed worker would have hardly been able to hit the coal at all.

When he was hooking from right to left, Edgar managed to get astonishing power behind his blows and the coal came crashing down in huge lumps. When he hooked from left to right he was unable to get the same force behind it and often had to prise the lumps out. After he had hacked his way through several feet of coal, Edgar was obliged to wriggle on top of the broken heap in order to get another crack at the face. Lying on top of the black rubble, he first picked up several large pieces from under his face and chest and passed them back to the drawer. Then he wriggled a little further forward into the hole he had made and commenced to kick back the rest of the rubble, like a dog making a hole at the bottom of the garden to bury his bone in.

Soon he had cleared himself enough space to be able to resume coal-cutting and the drawer got busy with the shovel, piling the coal up as far back as he could. Jake was sent back to fetch the tub and bring it down to the pile of broken coal, so they could fill it. To do this, they took three or four planks out of the front of the tub to enable them to get the coal in, since the top was scraping the roof. The drawer used the shovel and Jake picked up medium sized lumps in his hands and heaved them in after the shovelfuls. The air was filled with the fine dust and Jake coughed from time to time. He did not feel tired now that he had no crawling to do but he soon found that handling coal led to his hands getting covered in cuts and bruises. Gradually he began to feel his hands less and less and the cuts more and more, but he knew that he had not been so happy in months.

When the tub was full, it was Jake's turn to push it back to the shunt and put it on the main line for the pony to fetch. The drawer came back with him, pushing alongside. He showed him where to place the tub on the line and how to keep it in position using wedges, called scotches, rammed under the wheels. After that they went back to see how Edgar was getting on, taking with them another empty tub. Edgar, meanwhile, had brought down another impressive heap of rubble and was sitting on it drinking cold tea. Jake and the drawer had brought their tommy-tins in the empty tub and the three of them squatted in a triangle, silently eating their bacon, cheese, bread and coal dust. Jake enjoyed it. Edgar gave him a swig of cold, bitter tea and told him to remember to bring his own the next day. Jake wondered how he was going to brew it so bitter. They went back to work.

Jake had to take back the second tub on his own. At first he could not budge it, but once the drawer had given him a start he found that by leaning right forward, getting his feet firmly dug in and his head right down and pushing for all he was worth without letting up for a second, he could just manage to keep it on the move. There was a slight up-gradient and the only time he let up for a moment to try and get a better foot-hold the tub stalled on him and he had to suffer the humiliation of calling for the drawer to come and help him get a second start. On the third tub he made no mistake, and kept on scuffling whether his feet slipped or not.

After another dose of tea, Edgar gathered his forces for a fourth and final tub's worth and rested while the drawer loaded it up. He was still a bit short, so Edgar went back to it for another ten minutes and Jake and the drawer scraped the floor clean to make the tub up. By this time they were all tired, particularly Edgar, stripped to the waist and gleaming with sweat. Jake took the tub back and the two men followed slowly, bringing lamps, clothes and tommy-tins with them.

The pony was waiting at the shunt together with the pony-boy – a lad two or three years older than Jake – and another youth whose function it was to help push the tubs up the slope. Such workers are called thrutchers. Jake lashed on his tubs in the manner he had been shown and the pony-boy led off. Jake and the thrutcher lined up behind the back tub and pushed. The pony was in good shape and Jake did not find the thrutching too hard, although it seemed an incredibly long way back to the shaft. There runners-in took over and Jake had done for the day. He waited for Edgar and the drawer to come up and they entered the cage together. By the time they emerged from the pit-head it was half past four and dark. Jake realised that he would not see daylight again until the following Sunday morning.

For the next ten years Jake learned his trade, 10 to 12 hours a day and six days a week. Going to bed every night at nine and sleeping all Sunday morning as well meant that his social life was non-existent. Apart from a Sunday afternoon walk or fishing expedition with Tom, the pit was his whole life. Around the pit revolved the hopes, ambitions, disappointments and drama of his youth. On the whole, he was very happy. Down the mine he suffered no setbacks. It was generally recognised early on that he could work the back off anybody his own age and in the years that followed he was constantly in the thick of it. He skipped soft jobs such as leading ponies and minding doors and when he had collected enough scars on his hands lashing-on and helping drawers, he passed straight on to serious thrutching on two-scotch slopes where strength and stamina were needed and where he soon got his nose broken when a tub came back on him. He did not bother to have his nose seen to until the end of the shift and the amount of coal dust which got under the broken skin left him with a long blue scar down the bridge – the envy of his brother Tom for years, until he, too, got a bigger one over the left eye-brow when somebody caught him a glancer with a pick.

When he was fourteen, Jake had a year as a runner-in with more responsibility, but there was too little action and soon he was down in the workings again as a packer. Packers would go round in groups of three or four, packing into holes in the walls shovelfuls of coal dust lying loose on the floor. Good hard packing made the mine so much safer. It was a hard and monotonous job and the worst of all for getting coal dust in the lungs. From packing he went on to datelling. Datellers usually came down on the afternoon shift with the purpose of making the roof safe after the excavations of the morning. They pack, put up pit props, clear the floor and have the workings in shape for the next shift. While he was a dateller Jake covered a lot of ground down several mines in the Wigan area and saw many of the various aspects of mining. He saw how much coal could be got when the roof was high enough and how incredibly difficult working could be in 20 inches. He saw dry and hot workings where miners had to be constantly drinking and he saw others so damp that the men were continually rained on. He learned to watch out for gas and to listen for the creak of props indicating an imminent fall. He learned how to shield himself from dropping coal and where to run when the lot came down. He saw men killed by tubs and learned to keep off the track on a steep gradient. During this time he grew and hardened, taking knocks without complaining, and when he turned seventeen the boss put him straight on the coalface as a miner, confident that he would soon be filling tubs faster than any other man he had.

It took Jake ten days to learn how to handle the pick to his best advantage and after that he began to turn out coal like a machine. The first three drawers they put to work with him could not stand the pace and were all but buried under the pile of coal. Finally they found him a strong and experienced drawer named Hitchen, who had been a good coal-getter himself in his younger days. Hitchen was glad to team up with Jake when the latter announced that he was willing to go halves with his drawer when they paid him for the coal he had hewn. There were two possible arrangements between a miner and his drawer. Either the miner could pay him a flat rate per shift and take the rest himself, or he could go half and half on what they earned. Greedy miners usually made a flat guarantee and then worked like horses to make their own money, although this policy could backfire if the workings were difficult and they did not get enough coal. A hard-working miner with a good output naturally benefited by paying a guarantee instead of sharing. Jake, however, having decided it was no use paying a man a guarantee and then burying him, stuck to his arrangement with Hitchen, who was undoubtedly the fastest drawer in the pit. The result was that before Jake was 18 the pair of them had broken all records for getting coal that the pit had bothered to keep and they consistently took home pay packets twice as thick as those of their colleagues.

Tom, who went down the pit on his tenth birthday, followed largely in Jake's footsteps. While they were boys, Jake was always ahead of Tom in jobs and pay, but the younger brother did not mind as long as he was getting dirty every day. They always worked on the same shift and very often in the same part of the mine. When he was 18, Tom was promoted to the face and from then on the two brothers hewed coal side by side whenever the face was wide enough for more than one man to work at.

Tom was the only miner in the pit who could rival his brother in output. When they were working together he would match Jake tub for tub and swing for swing, though Jake generally brought down bigger lumps through better aiming, and would usually be three or four minutes ahead on each tub. In build, they were somewhat different. Although they were both of medium height, Jake was noticeably broader in the shoulders but with the narrow waist and slim hips of an athlete. Tom was not so broad and slightly round-shouldered, with a thicker waist and heavier legs. His strength lay in his huge bones which were apparently unbreakable and which made him quite a heavy man. When fully clothed he appeared, with his narrow, bony face and round shoulders, a lighter man than Jake, who had broad cheekbones, strong neck and ruddier countenance, but in reality Tom was a stone heavier than his brother. Armed with a pick, he displayed brute strength and his special hard swings had a sound all of their own. Jake could swing viciously, too, but he achieved his results more by his athlete's timing and mobility. From a difficult horizontal position he could uncoil like a spring and hit the coal just where he wanted to. He put all his strength into his blows but he was crafty in their distribution and he was one of the few miners who could swing equally well in both directions. He never tried to put out more tubs than Tom and employed the three minutes he might have gained kicking back broken coal to help his drawer. They both made good money and their drawers, too, were happy.

CHAPTER 20

Jake Lewis 1861-1939

Jake and Tom Lewis remained inseparable throughout their adult life and mining careers. Whenever they moved house it was always simultaneous. After marriage they consistently rented houses next door to each other with one wall separating Jake's and Tom's bedrooms. One hour before their morning shift, Jake would knock half a dozen times on the wall and the sleepier Tom would rouse himself. After breakfast they would exit their respective front doors and tramp to the pit-head. After their early years at the Bare Bones, they worked down a number of pits in the Wigan districts, eventually settling to live in Garswood and finally in Ashton-in-Makerfield.

Two years to the day after his father's burial, Jake married Jane Heaton, a young lady from Garswood, daughter of another collier, Samuel Heaton. Both Jake and Jane were 21 years of age. They rented a house at 54, School Lane, Garswood. Dutifully, Tom took up residence at 53, School Lane. Both houses were substantial buildings, a far cry from the cramped accommodation at Rock Farm. It was just as well that they enjoyed adequate space, as five sons were born to Jake and Jane between 1883 and 1896. They were all known mono-syllabically – Bob, Jack, Sam, Dick and Tom. A baby girl, Mary Ellen, born after Tom, survived only a few days. Jake's brother Tom, on the other side of the wall, was equally prolific, producing (between 1887 and 1904) three sons (Robert, Jake and Sammy) and five daughters (Mary, Margaret, Edith, Charlotte and Minnie). Over in Pemberton, their oldest brother John also had seven children, with similar names – Mary, Edward, Robert, Sara, Edith, Thomas and Margaret. The Lewises stuck to their favourite names through thick and thin.

When the 19th century came to an end, the British Empire reached its zenith with a land area of 15 million square miles and continued domination of the world's principal sea routes and naval production. The British built huge railway networks in India, Argentina and Brazil and on all continents. If the sun never set on Her Majesty's realm, it was the production of coal that became the driving force behind social, political and economic reforms around the globe. Coal's importance in the military sphere became evident in the lead-up to and during the First World War, when the world's three major producers of coal – Britain, the United States and Germany, settled their differences through horrible slaughter over a four year period on the Somme and other battlefields in Belgium and Flanders. The immense U.S. coalfield, largely in Pennsylvania, was half the size of Europe. Pittsburgh surpassed Wigan in becoming the smokiest city in the world. While pitmen were kept out of the army for the first few years (to maintain production for the war effort), they later were called up and suffered losses comparable to the number in mine disasters at home. When Jake turned 50, in 1911, 2,000 pitmen were killed down the pit and 16,000 injured. Half a decade later, 50,000 Yorkshire miners found themselves in the trenches; 5,000 of them paid the ultimate sacrifice. All Jake's sons except Robert served in France. Fortunately, all survived the hostilities, though Dick had a few narrow escapes.

With his sons back on the railway, Jake carried on hewing monotonously through the 1920s, with Tom at his side. In 1920, £2.10s.0d was considered a reasonable wage; Jake often took home over £3 and had no difficulty making ends meet. Rents were low, food relatively cheap and all his sons were in employment after 1912. Jake was in

Jake Lewis   *Tom Lewis*

contact with miners' leaders over these years – a close friend was Stephen Walsh, a pitman who became M.P. for Ince and achieved political fame as Secretary of State for War in the first Labour government. Jake later acted briefly as a father figure to 14-year-old Joe Gormley, who was President of the National Union of Mineworkers from 1971-81. Though he had good relations with miners' leaders, and his own son, Robert, was actually the miners' agent for Wigan before becoming Mayor, Jake throughout his life exhibited minimal interest in the industry's politics. Having banned his children from going down the pit, he followed much more closely his son Robert's performance as a leading member of the Wigan Town Council and especially in the years when he was Wigan's Chancellor of the Exchequer.

Only in later years could I appreciate the extent and depth of my grandfather's sacrifice, toiling 65 years underground with hardly ever a day off, brief holidays and restricted leisure time, decade after decade. Yet he never indicated, to my father or myself, that he felt imposed upon. He had a steady job – all his life – in his eyes it was a good one, and one at which he excelled. He ate well and heartily, he had good relations with his brothers and children and he was loyal to his employers, who trusted him implicitly. Jake Lewis would be the last man to start a strike (corrected: it would be Tom after him) and the only time my father observed Jake to be grumpy for a protracted period was during the 1926 general strike which lasted seven months and achieved nothing for the strikers. Unable to work, my father and his friends passed their enforced leisure time holding boat races with matches in the streams. Jake attended the event once, saw his match come in last and stomped off in disgust. The rest of the strike he passed walking 10-15 miles a day, over the fields of Garswood, Billinge and Upholland, visiting relatives or other striking miners. He was 65 at the time – he found the physical inactivity unbearable. He put on a stone and a half in weight, but promptly shed it a week after returning to work.

In his last working years he was employed at Park Colliery, Ashton-in-Makerfield, about a mile from where he went to live. This colliery was popularly known as Stone's, the mine being owned by J. and R. Stone Ltd., who owned it right up to nationalisation in 1947. It was not as deep as most pits Jake had worked in (the No. 1 shaft was 170 yards). It suited Jake and Tom not only because of its proximity to Low Bank Road (nos. 46 and 48, of course) but on account of Jake's close relations with the manager, Harry Ploddy, with whom he had shared experiences for over 30 years.

In December 1932, when Jake was 71 years of age, a young lad named Joe Gormley started down Stone's as a lasher-on. He was assigned to the same workings as Jake, who knew him as an Ashton neighbour. He took the lad under his wing in a minor way, giving him some technical advice and other tips for his safety. Many years later, I used to meet Joe Gormley on the streets of Ashton – by then he was on his way to becoming a national figure in the mining community. He mentioned affectionately his encounters with my grandfather, referring specifically to his rough, independent nature, spiced with

Pit brow women at Stone's Park Colliery, Garswood, in 1900

ever-present humour. Stone's was a 'dry' pit where pitmen were con-stantly thirsty. Jake told Joe to clean a small piece of cannel and then suck it during the shift. I remember Jake as always pulling on a clay pipe, even when he rocked me on his knee, telling me pit stories. Still today I retain the sense of his presence – physical and mental warmth, sharp eyes, rough voice, manly smell.

Tom retired in 1933 at the age of 70. For the last two years he had been suffering from Parkinson's Disease. I well remember the quivering of his hand as he took me for short walks along Low Bank Rd. He had a gentler voice than Jake and was invariably courteous with women and soft with children. He succumbed to Parkinsons on 18 December 1935 at the age of 72. His older brother John had died the previous week on 11 December in Pemberton aged 81. It was a mournful period for the Lewises, as Jake's wife Jane died a few weeks later on 18 January 1936, aged 74.

In the midst of these family bereavements, Jake still enjoyed good health at 74 and carried on working as usual. In February, however,

Pit brow lassies from Park Colliery, Garswood

he broke up his home in Low Bank Road – he was now alone as all the boys were married. Dick, my father, and the one who resembled him most, asked him to live with us in nearby Whitledge Green, Ashton, and that is how I had the good fortune to see him every day of his last years and witness at close quarters the vitality of spirit and intense vigour of a 19th century Lancashire miner whose like would not be seen again. He came through our door every day at five o'clock, straight from the pit with black face, clattering clogs, empty tommy-tin and jaunty stride. His face invariably lit up when he saw me. Whether I deserved it or not, I was the apple of his eye. I was his seventh grandchild – there had been a gap of nearly 10 years after the sixth and of course he knew I would be the last. A bond developed between us which still holds me. He took me alone to Southport on a day out and let me spend a whole sixpence, he smuggled me fruit drops in defiance of my parents, he bounced me on his hard knees for an hour at a time, he told me pit stories and sang me a collection of raucous miners' songs, he squeezed my shoulders hard every night before he sent me to bed. I was always in awe of him with his gnarled brown hands, aquiline, twice-broken nose with blue scars, stern, eagle-like eyes and broad sloping shoulders. I also adored him.

He carried on working for six months after the triple family bereavement, complaining neither of loneliness nor fatigue. He still had a family, a job, a calling. One day in June 1936, he entered the kitchen at the usual hour, black-faced, relaxed, with a hint of seriousness. My father, mother and I were waiting with his tea and hot tub at the ready. I noticed he had brought his lamp home – usually it stayed at the pit-head. He put it on the kitchen table and tossed his flat cap onto a chair. Turning to my father he said suddenly:

"Ah gid Harry me cards today, Dick."
My father was thunderstruck.
"Tha what?"
"Ah towd Harry ah'd finished."
My father stared at him incredulously.

Park Colliery in the 1950s

"An what did Harry say?"
"He said ah'm not takin' thi cards, Jake, tha cawn't leave afoor
me – Ah'm three year owder than thee."
"An what dit say?"
"Ah towd 'im it wuz no use, ah wuz givin' 'im me cards."
My father still was incredulous, but there was a hint of relief in
his mien.
"An what made thee think of finishin'?"
My grandfather looked at the back of his hands and then his
clogs in silence. After a while he said simply:
"Ah thowt ah'd done enough, Dick."

And that's how it ended. There had been no hint in previous days
that Jake was thinking of retiring. He had spoken animatedly of a
new seam they were opening up and had sharpened his pick the week
before. My father, who chatted with him daily, was completely in

the dark. He supposed later that Jake, who had witnessed an elderly miner get injured a month before, had decided to quit while the going was good. He had never suffered a serious injury. We shall never know why he took his decision in the middle of his shift after 65 years of underground toil, which never seemed to bother him. One thing was certain: when Jake decided to do something, there was no going back. He never descended the mine after that day and I never again saw his familiar black face.

I enjoyed his natural ruddy looks for the next four years and was never far from his side. When I came home from school I headed for Ashton park, where he spent the afternoons surrounded by septuagenarian admirers, all of them pitmen, of course. After the customary fruit drop, he would give me his horny hand and drag me back to Whitledge Green where we would drink my mother's tea and wait for Dick to bike back from the railway in Bamfurlong or Ince.

Jake had never been ill in his life – he had even been spared such pitmen's ailments as silicosis, asthma, even rheumatism. One day, he

Mains Colliery

fell headlong at Ashton market and grumbled his way home with a sore knee. The doctor diagnosed cancer, which claimed him on 25 June 1939. He died as he had lived, facing his fate with courage. Dick was equally stoic – the 46 years I spent with him continually reminded me of old Jake's qualities and magnetism and I like to think that some of Robert Lewis of Mold rubbed off on me, too.

Appendices

Appendix A

Postscript I: The Twentieth Century

From the beginning of the 20th century until the 1926 strike, more than one million workers were employed by the British coal industry. In the USA, a forceful former miner of Welsh descent, John L. Lewis, had built up the UMW (Union of Mine Workers) into the nation's strongest union. In 1935, he launched the Congress of Industrial Organisations (CIO), which soon claimed hundreds of thousands of members. Lewis, a militant, rhetorical figure, quickly became the country's most powerful individual after Roosevelt, whose 1933 New Deal had sparked the resurgence of the UMW. Lewis was extremely popular with workers from all industries and retained his charismatic leadership until the Second World War. When, however, he led the miners out on strike during the war, he was quickly reviled by the American public.

In Britain, by contrast, the war halted job losses among miners (they had seen their workforce reduced by more than 250,000 from 1925 to 1940). The popularity gained by their contribution to the war effort and the election of Attlee's Labour government at the end of the war ushered in the long-wished-for nationalisation of the mines in 1947. For the next 10 years, the employment situation remained stable. At the end of the 1950s, Britain employed three times as many coal miners as America but only produced half as much coal, due to the disparity in thickness of coal seams and more modern U.S. machinery.

During the 1960s, demand for coal slumped in both countries as oil and gas took over as fuels for most industries, especially automobiles. In Britain, miners' wages lagged behind those in other occupations and they went on strike in January 1972 asking for a substantial increase. Prime Minister Edward Heath refused it and instituted a three day work week, but the new miners' leader, Arthur Scargill, used 'flying pickets' to race around the country to block access to coal the government had stockpiled. Heath appealed to the public, calling a general election, but Labour won by a narrow majority and the new premier, Yorkshireman Harold Wilson, was only too happy to settle with the miners.

The President of the NUM, Joe Gormley, who had worked at Stone's for two or three years with Jake Lewis, had been less militant than Scargill. He was of the opinion that the size and the future of coal mining in Britain and elsewhere would be determined by external forces outside his control. Joe simply fought for the best wages he could obtain for pitmen as long as the industry remained viable. Scargill, on the other hand, was determined to keep mines open at all costs.

This attitude led him into a head-on confrontation with Margaret Thatcher, who became Prime Minister in 1979. She noted that three-quarters of Britain's (nationalised) coal mines were running at a loss. A return to profitability would mean the closure of many pits and the laying off of tens of thousands of miners. She appointed Ian McGregor, a Scottish-American steel and coal executive, to put into effect such draconian measures. Scargill decided to take a stand and employed his usual tactics of initiating strikes, using flying pickets and engaging in stormy confrontations with the police. Thatcher refused to back down and clashes led to a day of violence in June 1984 where street battles led to 89 people being taken to hospital including Arthur Scargill and 37 police officers.

The dismantling of Wigan Pier

The following months were bleak ones for the striking miners. As many pitmen, especially in Nottinghamshire, drifted back to work, Thatcher remained resolute in her policies ("The lady is not for turning"). The strike collapsed in March 1985, after a final bitter, impassioned speech by the fiery Scargill. The writing was clearly on the wall concerning the industry's future. By 1986, fewer than 100,000 miners were at work in Britain; by 1990 only 50,000; today fewer than 5,000. What remained of the coal industry was, ironically, privatised in 1994. Outside the UK, the industry suffered a similar fate in France and Germany, albeit without protest from the miners. Though the US industry remains strong through increased modernisation, the work force dropped from 200,000 to 70,000. Over a million miners have been laid off in China.

The long mining traditions in Britain meant that miners and their relatives had a profound sense of kinship with the past. They felt centuries of hardship by their ancestors had cemented their identification with the profession. When a mining village saw their pit closed and witnessed the economic devastation that followed, their sense of togetherness, community and continuity was swept away. That is why the closure of a pit was resisted most stoutly, even desperately, not by the mine-owner, but by the pitmen and their families themselves.

Appendix B

Postscript II: The Future of Coal

In his memoirs, Joe Gormley points out that 400 years of coal reserves still lie under our feet in Britain. Alan Davies, the former curator of the Lancashire Mining Museum in Salford, asserts, in his book, 'The Pit Brow Women of the Wigan Coalfield', that the British coal mining industry and its communities were wiped out for purely political (not economic) reasons, this constituting one of the greatest crimes ever perpetrated against the English working classes.

What future role will coal play in the world at large and in Britain in particular? As a descendant of a family whose involvement in mining goes back to at least the 17th century, I am viscerally interested in this question, the answer to which would lend perspective to the historical relevance of the lives and careers of my grandfather, great-grandfather and hundreds of thousands of their contemporaries.

If they lived today, Robert and Jake Lewis would stand stunned at the evolution of the coal mining industry, the statistics of which leave anyone dazed. In 1864, near the peak of Robert Lewis's activity in Wigan, Britain produced 93 million tons of coal. Before his death, in 1880, production had risen to 154 million tons (North Wales two million tons) and the industry employed 500,000 men. If we compare these figures with the 2010 world annual production of *6 billion tons*, the British 19th century numbers seem puny. In reality, they were huge and crucial for their time. One does well to remember that, at that level of production, coal fuelled the Industrial Revolution and the needs of the enormous British Empire.

In the context of global warming and attempts at pollution reduction, coal has become again, not for the first time in its history, a dirty word. The increases in the worldwide consumption of coal are alarming:

India coal imports:	2008 – 36 million tons
	2009 – 60 million tons
USA exports to China:	2009 – 2,714 tons
	2010 – 6 million tons
Australia exports to China:	2008 – $508 million
	2010 – $5,600 million

Such figures suggest that the evolution of the coalmining industry is unstoppable, whatever politicians and environmentalists may think or do. There are several potent reasons for this. Firstly, the increase in the price of coal ($50 a ton in 2005, $114 a ton in 2010) makes it one of the world's most profitable growth sectors. Secondly, coal – with immense known reserves – is crucial to the planet's need for energy. Thirdly, although restrictions are placed on enterprises where coal is burned, these limitations are rarely applied where coal is dug up.

At the time of writing, Essar Energy, an energy company in Gujarat on the west coast of India, is planning to spend $6 billion on building eight coal-fired power stations. These will add tens of millions of tons of carbon to the atmosphere, but a spokesman for Essar said its customers on the subcontinent could not afford the extra costs associated with subsidising cleaner technologies. This development is likely to be repeated hundreds of times in locations like Gujarat, where 44% of households do not have any power at all.

China, by dint of necessity, has few qualms about consuming coal. A perennial coal exporter until 2009, she actually *imported* 150 million tons in 2011 – about the same amount as Japan, the long-time world leader. **We are talking about a trillion dollar industry, employing 43 million people**.

What does this scenario mean for Britain? We are sitting on 2.3 billion tons of our black mineral ("the riches beneath our feet"). In addition, we have 800 million tons of close-to-the-surface coal at our disposal. Will it be used? This country has been blessed with sources of energy. Our oil, however, is disappearing fast. The same applies to our natural gas. Nuclear power brings with it huge problems of waste disposal. Britain has only limited water for hydro-electric power. Gormley advocated a well-thought-out, coordinated national energy policy, certainly supported by social liberalism, but where, except for Scandinavia, New Zealand and Canada can one be optimistic? Free market conservatism seems to offer no solution.

Fringe sources of power – tidal, solar, wind, geo-thermal, hydro-electric (favourites of environmentalists) are all to be exploited, but in Britain (and not only here) new technologies focused on coal may well provide the answer. Synthetic gas can be made from coal. Coal can be extracted by gasification, liquefaction or burned *in situ*. Coal can produce oil and 27 different by-products, from dyes to plastics. The investments required to make these new technological methods viable are unimaginably vast. Yet the cold countries of the world have no choice. Without energy they will perish. There is no other option.

It may be implied that new technical means of extracting coal (including robotic devices) will eliminate or drastically reduce the *raison d'être* for miners. One hundred years from now, they might be looked upon as we now regard children sweeping Victorian chimneys. This is unlikely. As long as coal is mined, the men who have the skills of utilising machinery, moving forward with the coal faces, who possess the courage to face the hazards of the most dangerous of professions, will be present in what many of us see as an inevitable renaissance of the coalmining industry.

Note on Gladstone

(following remarks in the Foreword)

In fact, another, and more illustrious, copy exists in the Gladstone Library in nearby Hawarden. This beautiful book, bound in luxurious green leather, was the personal copy of William Gladstone, the founder of the library, who was also four times Prime Minister of Great Britain. This remarkable statesman, who served as Premier longer than any other person, was greatly interested in the writing of Daniel Owen (a few miles from his residence) and the activities of Robert Lewis, the hero of 'Rhys Lewis'.

William Gladstone (1809-1898) first entered Parliament in 1832 – the year of Robert's birth – and was initially a disciple of High Toryism, opposing the abolition of slavery and factory legislation. He defined one of his main political goals as the defence of the Church of England and even proposed the removal of Non-conformists and Roman Catholics from government office. He soon changed these views after associating with Peel and later, when engaging with electoral reform, he gained popularity with the masses, who called him the "People's William". On a tour of the North in 1862, when he

Rhys Lewis' autobiography.

went down the Tyne, "all the country went to greet him... men stood in the blaze of chimneys; the roofs of factories were crowded; colliers came up from the mines;...he heard cheers no other English minister ever heard...the people were grateful to him, and rough pitmen who never approached a public man before, pressed round his carriage by thousands...to shake hands with Mr. Gladstone as one of themselves."

Gladstone was a great orator and knew how to speak to workers. In 1869 – the year of the Mold Riot – he answered a complaint from an unemployed miner:

"The only means which have been placed in my power of "raising the wages of colliers" has been by endeavouring to beat down all those restrictions upon trade which tend to reduce the price to be obtained for the product of their labour and to lower the taxes on the commodities they require for use or consumption".

Later, he declared:

"It is a lamentable fact if, in the midst of our civilisation, and at the close of the 19th century, the workhouse is still all that can be offered to the industrious labourer at the end of a long and honourable life...I say that until society is able to offer to him at the end of a blameless life something better...it will not have discharged its duties to its poorer members".

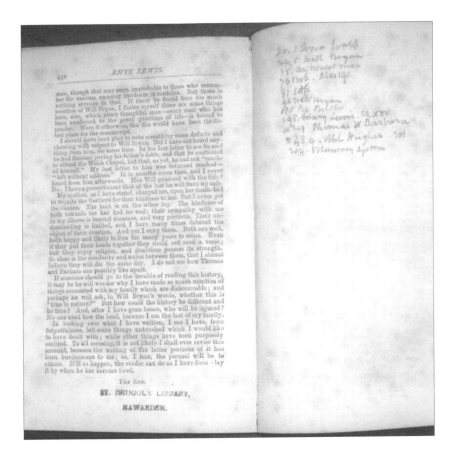

ABOVE: *The final page of Rhys Lewis' autobiography, with Gladstone's notes.*

RIGHT: *Gladstone's notes with reference to Mary Lewis, enlarged.*

Gladstone later supported London dockers in their 1889 strike, he encouraged enfranchisement to all normal beings (Queen Victoria was seen displeased at this), and he often said Englishmen must be given rights because it was *just*.

Though many of his remarks were appreciated in nearby Mold, Gladstone was ambivalent in his support of the pitmen when they rebelled. Hence his keen interest in Daniel Owen. I have read his personal, pencilled annotations in the margins of his copy of *'Rhys Lewis'*. They are most numerous in the pages describing the speeches and actions of Robert Lewis. The angry pitmen of Mold were only five miles from Gladstone's Hawarden Manor – perhaps too close for comfort.

Appendix D

Clogs

While clogs could be formidable weapons for individuals who engaged in 'porrin', they were, of course, normal footwear in Wigan for miners and their families, as well as for most people of the working classes. In the Scholes, clogs were worn by all and sundry six days a week (sometimes on Sundays) outdoors, in pubs and shops, at work (always down the pit).

There were three types of clogs – lace-ups with leather laces favoured by men and big lads, low-down clasped ones worn by younger boys (or old men) and slightly more elegant ones, for girls and women, with a dainty strap across the top. The leather uppers were attached to wooden soles (alder or sycamore) shaped to the foot. Wiganers regarded them as healthier than shoes, though they had to be broken in over a period. Women often used "rubber irons" but males clattered along with noisy metal clog-irons. In icy weather boys would engage in "slorrin'" – sliding along a "slorr" at great speed. On frozen flashes some lads could skate along the inside irons almost as fast as a real ice-skater on skates.

As I grew up in a mining area, my early waking hours were invariably accompanied by the deafening clattering of clogs as dozens of pitmen made their way to work. The noise would rise to a crescendo over a half hour period. My grandfather walked and worked in clogs and, when annoyed, often threatened to "porr" individuals, though I never saw him carry out the threat. He had a red leather pair with shiny brass toe-caps for Sundays. He wore them everywhere (shops, barber's, parks) but not in chapel.

Clog dancing was popular in the 19th and early 20th century. It may well have been the forerunner of tap dancing. Clogs (or sabots) were used in other parts of Europe (Holland, France) but were more ubiquitous in Wigan than in any other town.

Acknowledgment given to Tom Heaton in his article on "Clogs" in the magazine "Past Forward" (April-July 2011) (Wigan Heritage Service).

Pit Lassies

"The Wigan Tippler"
(As told by a pit brow lass circa 1880)

It's used to unload tubs intae barges waitin' ont' cut. Tubs
full o' coal, that we will uv sorted, and reet ard work it is!
US Pit Brow Lasses are responsible for "shakin" the
coal (getting rid of the stones) on a Shaking Screen, and
sorting it – mostly by hand, into different sizes.
The coal comes down a conveyor belt. There are six of us
Lassies to a belt. We work hard – six in the morning 'til six
in the evening weekdays, finishing at two on Saturdays.
Our muscles are bigger than most of the men's. At night
we soak our hands in cold tea to soothe the cracks.
We wear clogs, shawls and aprons made from sacking.
But it's our trousers we're known for. You see, women in
trousers are frowned on – people think we're immoral.
Machinery's startin t'replace us Lassies.
But they aren't a patch on us."

Taken from a placard at Wigan pier

The term 'pit-lassies' refers to the women who were employed down or around the mines in large numbers during the 19th and early 20th centuries. After the 1842 Coal Mines Act prohibited women from working underground, it was used more specifically to describe female *surface* workers.

Women supporting men in mining activities was nothing new; historical records refer to female miners in Egypt, South America and Germany over the course of many centuries. That the pit-lassies achieved fame in 19th century Britain was due to their large numbers, as pits mushroomed to service the factories and mills of the Industrial Revolution. By far the largest concentration of female mine-workers was in south Lancashire and the name 'pit-lassie' became almost synonymous with girls and women from Wigan. From c. 1850 to the outbreak of the First World War these cheerful, sturdy females were

Pit brow lassies

A brief rest

celebrated in hundreds of photographs and drawings published in *The London Illustrated News*, *The Graphic*, *The Pictorial World* and other national papers and magazines, startling the majority of the British public hitherto completely unaware of the extent and hardship of brutal underground toil.

Apart from the horrific working conditions endured by women labouring underground, one of the main factors of interest of these illustrations was the colourful garb they dressed in. A.J. Munby (a 19th century academic and minor poet who took an interest in pit-girls) describes their typical attire in one of his diaries, August 1859:

"The costume of these girls and women is always the same, and a good useful one it is. A hooded bonnet of padded cotton, pink, blue or black. A blue striped shirt, open at the breast, a waist-coat of cloth, generally double breasted – but ragged and patched throughout. Fustian or corduroy or sometimes blackcloth trousers, patched with all possible materials except the original one, and stout clog shoon, brassclipped on their bare feet. Round the waist is tucked a petticoat of striped cotton, blue and black, rolled up as a

joiner rolls his apron: it is never let down, and is perfectly useless –
only retained as a symbol of sex."

This mode of attire, with occasional original or flattering variations, persisted in the Wigan area even during the 1930s in my own experience and the photograph on page 226 of girls I met on going down Mains Colliery, Bamfurlong in 1950, shows vestiges of the old style, though considerably diluted.

Pit-lassies varied in age from 13 to 70. On the surface, the work of sorting, washing and breaking up pieces of coal was exhausting, incessant, occasionally dangerous and freezing in winter. Girls wore

Lassies' pay queue

fingerless gloves, hands were numb in cold weather, bled frequently, coal dust was ingrained in fingers and also caused dermatitis. As experiments with underground toilets had proved a failure in the pits, human excretion was sent up the shaft and along the belt with the coal – just one more job hazard for the lassies who would shout "Here come th'ashes o't roses" when they could smell it nearing their screens. Shifts could be seven to nine hours long and many women tramped two or three miles back and forth from home. There was no cover; on rainy days, lassies worked in soaking wet shirts, trousers and petticoats without respite. They endured the harshness of their job with the knowledge that pit wages, miserable though they were, were considerably higher than mill wages. Nobody wanted to lose her job.

This last truth was laid bare when, in the years following the Coal Mines Act, pressure from various sources was applied to eliminate women from the mining industry. In 1911, when the Coal Mines Regulation Bill was being read in Parliament threatening to exclude women from surface work, 47 pit-brow women from Wigan formed a deputation to go to London and paraded through Whitehall in their clogs, shawls, pit pants and petticoats, supported by Sam Woods, the Mayor, and Stephen Walsh, the M.P. for Wigan, the latter inciden-tally being a close friend of Jake Lewis, at that time in his 50th year.

The proposals for exclusion were attacked with vigour. How could one threaten a certain section of women's livelihood in this manner? Were there to be no more women employed to harvest crops or to pick hops? What about milkmaids?

In the end, though their numbers were decimated, pit-lassies sur-vived in Wigan even after the nationalisation of the mines in 1947. At all events, they were colourful figures in the history of English industry. In 1911 more than 5,000 women were engaged in the work. Most of them were happy in their jobs, considering the surface work, at least, to be healthier than that in mills or factories. Even women prohibited from working underground defied the law by dressing as men and sneaking down the pit under the noses of supervisors. Mineowners often turned a blind eye. Some women gave birth down the pit; one brought her newborn to the pit shaft in her skirt. Pit-lassies were characterized by resoluteness, independence and grit. Few were gloomy; generally they laughed together during their shifts and in hard times (e.g. strikes) they showed an unbreakable community spirit. Their work could pass through several generations.

One day in March 1865, A.J. Munby walked from Wigan in the direction of St. Helens, and passed through Billinge to inspect pits. Near Sammy Stock's pit he spoke to "a respectable man" in the coal office asking for advice. The man told him to visit Sammy Stock's and Munby interviewed a 17-year old girl there, whom he described as an attractive and thoroughly worthy individual. In his words:

"I was struck by her brisk and easy air, and stopped to talk with her, and she seemed glad enough to have someone to talk to. Her name was Margaret Roughley, and her age 17; she has an elder sister working on the pit brow close by. This Margaret was a well

grown girl: her collier bonnet was tilted over her eyes, which spar-
kled under lashes thickly clogged with coal dust: her face was very
black, but also singularly expressive and intelligent: her arms were
bare: she has a woollen comforter round her neck: a loose patched
shirt, looking very thin and cold: a short baglike apron of sackcloth;
short fustian trousers, only reaching to the calf; grey stockings, and
big clog shoon, whose iron soles were turned up at the toe like a
Chinaman's boot. Margaret laughed a boyish laugh, and showed
her white teeth, like Irish diamonds set in black bog oak. The,
she leaned her back against the earth of the cutting, crossed her
legs easily, tucked her hands under her "barmskin" and looked
straight at me, talking away for ten minutes as gaily and freely as
if she had always known me. She spoke the broadest Lancashire,
and spoke it so fast that I scarce follow her. She didn't dislike this
work, and although now she only earned 1/ a day while some broo
wenches earn 1s/2d she hoped soon to be "raised" from 10p a day
already. She could not read: yet she was one of the brightest and
most interesting girls I ever saw: as sharp and lively as a London
street boy, yet with nothing impudent or unfeminine about her.
True, her dress and manners were those of a lad; she jumped and
ran, and hitched up her trousers, like one who knew nothing about
petticoats, but in all her words and ways there was an artless
simplicity and truthful frankness that was thoroughly girlish. She
had humour too, and wit beyond her years; she was always saying
something comic and then merrily laughing at her own conceit:
she laughed at her grotesque attire: 'such queer old clothes as we
wear' said she 'ragged ones that folk gie us – our brothers old coats
and britches – anything does to work at pit in: but we wear our
breeches always, yo know, 'cept Sundays – and nice and warm they
are too!' "

Roughley is a Billinge name – I was born in Billinge and knew
her descendants. An even more striking coincidence is that the
"respectable man" Munby refers to was almost certainly my *other*

Sorting the coal

great-grandfather, James Parr, who was checkweighman at Sammy Stock's pit in 1865. Moreover, his wife, Susannah Parr – my great-grandmother – was a pit-lassie at the same pit, renowned for her fine figure and graceful movements.

Appendix F

A Tale of Two Mines

In 1950, while I was still at university, two of my classmates from Ashton and Haydock, Harry Wagstaff and Ronnie James, started work as pitmen. After nationalisation in 1947, many mines were closing and I was anxious to go down one while there was still a chance. My father, who supervised coal wagon transports from Mains Colliery, Bamfurlong, near Wigan, was able to arrange half a day's descent for me and my friend Bob Bradley. We went down with a bunch of pitmen on the morning shift at 6:30.

I had read Jake's description of his impressions of his first day down the pit. They were uncannily similar to my own – the strange behaviour of the cage, the hot, blankety air, the sullen, bored young trappers, the miles-long walk to the face, the eerie lighting, the musty smells, the ubiquitous pit props and tubs, the bare-chested black-faced colliers, above all the agonizing crawl on one's knees, in a low seam, for the last hundred yards to the coal face. Bob and I were fascinated and exhausted at the same time. Some miners ignored us, hewing viciously without interruption. The drawers joked with us, slaving away nevertheless. The activity was relentless, though Bob and I could do little but watch and gawp. I thought of Jake keeping up this breakneck pace for 60-odd years.

Surface workers, Mains Colliery, 1950

We came up after four hours, accompanied by one of the over-lookers. On the surface, we were greeted by a cheerful, wise-cracking bunch of pit-lassies, all of whom knew my father well. They giggled at our exhausted state, plied us with hot cups of tea, flirted with us as I took their picture. I would say they loved men, their work, and life in general: they were a sight for sore eyes. Bob and I, with our college airs, were novelties for them and, for a while, they would not let us go – they had fun with us. Sixty years later, I still feel their warmth, sincerity, *joie de vivre* and uncomplicated exuberance.

*   *   *

A few years later, I spent six hours down the Wieliczka salt mine in Krakow, Poland. This is 372 metres deep and nine centuries old. For me, there were some interesting comparisons. Salt mines, like coal mines, are dangerous. Methane gas explosions and periodic flooding killed the workers just as in Lancashire or Wales. Death was so common that the mine had an underground chapel where mass was said every morning before the shift. Salt mined underground is black or green in colour, not white. Miners carve beautiful sculptures

Carved and polished

Portrait in coal

or scenes in the chalk, just as Wigan pitmen did with cannel coal. Probably the Poles were more skilful or motivated. Their salt-carved 'Last Supper' is masterful. One of the huge chambers had a beautiful chandelier with salt crystals. Rock salt gnomes can be seen here and there.

Salt was mined at Wieliczka from the Middle Ages until 1996. There was one great difference between the working conditions of Krakow mines and those in Britain's coal pits. Our miners breathed

A Krakow chamber

The Last Supper

coal dust and generally expired in their forties and fifties. Salt miners breathe salt – which is healthy – and many lived till their eighties and nineties.

APPENDIX G

Mining is still Dangerous

Robert Lewis and his contemporaries faced annihilation daily from mishaps ranging from flooding in Wales to frequent devastating explosions in the gaseous Lancashire mines. In the 19th century, much mining equipment was primitive, defective or carried great risk with its use. One has to suppose that one hundred years of improvements in the 20th century has made pitmen's lives safer.

This is only true to some extent. While these last chapters have been written, five fatal mining accidents – three of them major – have taken place. In North Yorkshire's Kellingley Colliery, Gerry Gibson (a skilled, experienced miner) was killed by a roof fall, as a trapped colleague was pulled out alive. After medical attention, the colleague immediately re-descended the mine to show rescuers the way. Earlier in the month, four miners met their death in the flooding at the Gleision Colliery in Pontardawe in South Wales. In China, 26 pitmen were killed in an explosion and another 11 still trapped and feared dead.

The mining communities of the world (and many others) had their eyes glued to television to witness the spectacular rescue of 33 Chilean miners who remained trapped for a record 69 days 700 metres underground below Chile's Atacama desert. The dramatic rescue operation

Wigan Tech (now the Town Hall)

involved unimaginable tension over a 10-week period as trapped men, relatives and mine officials wrestled with crucial problems of food, sustenance, cleanliness, discipline and psychological stress. There was a happy ending as narrow bore-holes just enabled all the men to reach the surface, albeit in claustrophobic capsules.

The following disaster, in New Zealand, ended in catastrophe. Twenty-seven men were trapped two and a half kilometres from the pit shaft, after five had been dragged out to safety. The nature of the explosion, and the certain knowledge that a huge amount of gas still lurked in the workings, prevented an otherwise willing rescue team from descending. After an agonizing waiting period, while all New Zealand including the Prime Minister – present over the shaft – held their breath and hoped that the trapped men's oxygen supply would be sufficient to save them, another sickening explosion was heard which sealed the fate of the victims below. Most of the bodies may never be recovered. Some relatives expressed the wish that the mine be closed forever and a memorial erected over the shaft.

A poignant footnote to the disaster is that it took place near Greymouth, which gives it a slight connection with Wigan. Cecil Mountford, a New Zealand rugby league player who achieved great fame playing for Wigan, originated from Greymouth, where he was the second son of a mining family, and actually studied for a Mine Manager's Certificate in Wigan Mining & Technical College.

Additional Photographs

Jake's five sons (from left to right): Tom, Bob, Dick, Jack, Sam

Downall Green Methodists (Jake and Tom, front row, left and centre)

Tom, Jake and John Lewis

Jake's fourth son, Dick, aged 16

Robert Lewis, Mayor of Wigan, in full regalia

Robert Lewis receiving the Freedom of the Borough

Robert Lewis, Mayor of Wigan

Jake, aged 50

Robert Lewis III

A tough crowd

Glossary of Mining Terms

Back-shift	The afternoon or evening shift in coalmining
Backening	Where a collier is working some distance from the coal-tub and it is necessary for him to throw the coal in a heap behind him to be put into the tub
Bait	A light meal
Bait-time	A break for food
Banksman	A man employed at the pit top to take charge of the colliery cage
Bass	Impure, rocky coal, especially that which is left behind after domestic burning
Belts	Moving belts or screens at the surface of a colliery where coal was sorted; conveyor belts underground in a coal-mine
Blackdamp	A mixture of nitrogen and carbon dioxide which can result in oxygen deficiency in a coal-mine
Blowing	Shotfire in a colliery
Bobbin	The turn-wheel on a self-acting incline in a coal-mine

Bogie	A flat-bottomed truck for man-riding in a colliery
Braid	An estimated stretch of uncut coal underground
Brattice	A thick material used underground in coal-mining to direct the airflow
Breaking in	Cutting a vertical niche in the coal-face
Brow	An underground incline in a coal-mine
Bucket pump	A pump containing a piston fitted with "flap" valves working in a vertical barrel
Bullion	A section of unstable roof in a coal-mine
Bummer	The boss in charge of a group of men at a longwall face in a coal-mine
Bunton or baulk	A wooden beam in a shaft
Butterfly	The detaching hook on a colliery cage which in the event of the cage being overwound prevents the cage from falling back down the shaft
Butty	A workmate in a coal-mine
Butty-system	A system of payment where a foreman or chargeman receives the wages for his whole team. The wage was then divided up by mutual agreement
Canch	An area of roof left in after the coal has been extracted. It is subsequently removed to widen a passage
Canch or ripping	Stone taken from the roof or floor of a seam in road-ways in order to make height
Cannel	A type of coal. There is a coal-seam known as the Cannel Mine
Cap	A wooden top for a pit prop
Capstan engine	Engine geared to lift heavy weights
Cased-off	A place fenced off because of excess methane

Chariot	A special wagon used to transport rails, props etc. The wagon was made of wood with one or both ends missing to permit it to carry long loads
Chartermaster	The person in charge of a group of men at the coal-face, especially under the butty sytem
Check	A numbered disc used in coal-mining as a record of those actually underground. Checks were handed back on emerging from underground
Check-weighman	The person who checks and weighs the coal tubs
Chocks	A wooden support system for the roof
Cleat	A vertical facing or parting in a seam in two directions generally at right angles to each other
Cocker-bar	A pit prop used to support an underground roadway in a coal-mine
Cockering	A specialised form of timbering in a coal-mine
Cockermegs	See "cockering"
Cod-wagoning	Running tubs for a distance in a continuous relay by a team of boys
Collier	A coal getter or hewer
Colliery	A place entered by a shaft rather than by an inclined entrance
Crab	A portable windlass used in haulage near the coalface in a colliery
Cradle	A structure like a sledge for hauling coal
Crump	A small gas explosion in a colliery
Crutch	A small wooden stool or support used by colliers to support themselves whilst hand-hewing coal
Dataller	Skilled miner paid by the day who carried out roadway repairs and other general work

Day-eye	A type of coal-mine entered by an incline; the view looking back up the incline towards the surface
Day-hole	A day-eye or drift mine, especially into a hillside
Daylad	A drawer waiting his turn for coal-getting
Dayload	Tubs of coal filled by a dayman. No piece work was paid for these loads. They were usually filled by men tidying up the pit
Det box	A small leather box which was fastened to a man's belt in which detonators for explosives were carried
Dialer	A colliery surveyor using a surveyors dial
Dicky	A kind of pit pony
Dinting	To remove part of the floor in a coal-mine
Dip-drawer	The person who draws tubs up an incline (dip) to the main haulage
Dirt	The seat-earth of a coal-seam
District	An area in a mine being worked
Dog	A safety device hung on the back of the last tub on rope worked inclines. Should the rope break, the dog would dig into the floor and throw the tubs off the rails
Donkey	A clog sole with the heel removed, used by colliers as a kind of ski in order to slide down the rails into the workings
Donkey-engine	A small compressed air engine for haulage
Downcast shaft	The shaft down which fresh air is drawn
Drawer	One who draws tubs in a coal-mine
Drawing	The job of taking full tubs from the collier and returning with empty tubs for refilling
Drift	A tunnel or a road in or to a seam

Duck-lamp	A paraffin lamp used by daymen and banksmen in tunnels near the surface of a colliery
Falling-up	The collapse of a roof in a coal-mine, often blocking the passage
Fault	A geological dislocation in the strata
Fire	To shot-fire in a coal-mine, often used as a warning shouted immediately prior to shot-firing
Fireman	A foreman in a colliery usually in charge of the safety of an underground district. Originally it was the responsibility of the fireman to check for the presence of methane gas by holding a brand of fire in the upper part of a working or passageway. Hence the term fireman
Flat rods	Horizontal rods generally at the surface which transmit the motion of a pumping engine
Gang	A number of colliers working together
Gang-riding	Man-riding on a set of coal-tubs
Gateway	The passage leading from a place to the haulage road
Getter	A coal-heaver, a collier
Gin	A winding or other machine generally worked by horses; a self-acting incline in a coal-mine
Goaf, gob or waste	The collapsed excavated space behind the coal face supports
Hew	To mine coal
Hewer	A collier
Holing-out	Undercutting coals with a pick in such a way as to enable the coal to fall when the temporary supports are removed
Hooker-on	A person who pushes tubs into the workings from a colliery cage

Hoppet	A large iron bucket for lifting men and materials in the colliery shaft
In-by	The passageways or routes leading away from the downcast shaft of a coal-mine. The opposite to out-by
Iron-man	An early compressed-air coal-cutting machine
Jabber	A pneumatic pick used in a colliery
Jackbit	A light meal usually taken underground in a coal-mine
Jib	(of coal cutting machine) The flat steel arm around which travels the cutting chain with its picks
Kibble	A large iron bucket for lifting in a colliery shaft
Landing	A roadway off the main haulage in a mine
Lashing on	Attaching a coal-tub to a haulage system chain or rope
Leg	A pit prop
Ley	The first layer of coal above dirt
Linesman	A man who sets lines for underground surveying
Longwall	A method of mining where the coal is extracted in one operation without the use of pillars
Main and tail	Haulage engine with two drums where the ropes connect round pulleys to the front and rear of a train of tubs. Used on undulating or flat roads
Mangle	A small windlass for haulage
Manhole	Refuge to let tubs pass
Mouthing	Entrance to a seam or tunnel from a shaft
Nog	A tally placed on a tub leaving the pit
Nuts	Small pieces of coal
Outcrop or crop	The position where a coal seam reaches the surface

Overlooker	A foreman in a coal-mine
Packs	Stone and dirt walls in a mine, used to support the roof
Pisser	Water continually running off the roof of mine workings
Pit-bank	The place where a cage unloads at the surface of the pit
Pit-eye	Point below ground in shaft where tubs are loaded at the cage
Plug rod	A vertical rod attached to the beam of an engine which operates through tappets the steam and exhaust valves of the engine
Powder-monkey	Assistant to shot-firer
Pump or spear rods	The vertical rods in a shaft, attached to the end of the engine beam, which actuate the pumps
Pusher-on	A shunt minder
Rigs	A geological fault
Ripping	A section of roof or roadway that has to be removed by blasting
Rods	Cage guide-rods in a shaft
Ruck	A colliery spoil-heap
Scotch	A hooked pin or a wedge for braking tubs
Scufter	A man who cleans out the cut made by a coal-cutting machine
Shaft pillar	Coal left for the support of the shaft
Sough	A drainage tunnel
Sprag	Wooden wedge for braking tub
Straitwork	Narrow stalls in pillar work

Strip	A length of colliery rail
Tappets	Levers operating the valve gear of a steam engine
Thrutcher	Person pushing tubs up inclines
Tram	A long-bottomed wagon used in a pit
Upcast shaft	Shaft through which foul air is expelled from the mine by the use of a fan or (in former times) a furnace
Winder	Man who winds cages
Working (roof)	Unstable

References

Aspin, C. (1969), 'Lancashire, The First Industrial Society'.

Bailey, Catherine (2007), 'Black Diamonds', Penguin Books, London.

Bolton Chronicle, 31 July 1869

Brown, Sheila, 'A Brief History of Stubshaw Cross', Stubshaw Cross Residents Group, Wigan.

Cannon, Olga and Anderson, J.R.L. (1973), 'The Road From Wigan Pier', Camelot Press, London.

Challinor, Raymond (1972), 'The Lancashire and Cheshire Miners', Frank Graham, Newcastle-upon-Tyne.

Davies, Alan (2010), 'Coal Mining in Lancashire & Cheshire', Amberley Publishing, Stroud, Gloucester.

Fletcher, Mike (2002), 'Black Gold & Hot Sand', Carnegie Publishing, Lancaster.

Forman, Charles (1978), 'Industrial Town', Cameron & Tayleur, London.

Freese, Barbara (2002), 'Coal – a Human History', Perseus Books.

Gormley, Joe (1982), 'Battered Cherub', Hamish Hamilton Ltd, London.

Griffiths, Jenny and Mike (2001), 'The Mold Tragedy of 1869', Gwasg Carreg Gwalch, Llanrwst, Wales.

Gruffydd, Ken Lloyd, 'The Argoed Hall Colliery Disaster of 1837'.

Hannavy, John and Lewis, Roy (1982), 'The Maypole, Diary of a Colliery Disaster', Wigantech Publications, Wigan.

Heaton, Tom (2011), 'Clogs', Past Forward magazine, Wigan Heritage Service.

Lane, J., Anderson, D., 'Mines and Miners of South Lancashire 1870-1950', Greenslates, Parbold, Lancashire.

Lewis, Richard D. (1976, 1985, 2009), 'The Billingers', Riversdown Publications Ltd and Transcreen Publications Ltd.

Morris, Delyth and Williams, Paul, 'Coalmining', Buckley Community Heritage Environmental Local Project.

Nadin, Jack (2008), 'Lancashire Mining Disasters', The History Press Ltd.

'Portraits of 19th Century Lancashire Miners Leaders', Working Class Movement Library, Salford, Lancashire.

Simm, Geoff and Winstanley, Ian (1990), 'Mining Memories', St. Helens Metropolitan Borough Council.

Tattum, George (2007), 'The Spirit of Mold', Landmark Publishing, Ashbourne, Derbyshire.

'The Mold Riots', (1991), Clwyd Record Office, Hawarden.

'The Mold Tragedy', (1869), Wrexham Advertiser.

Wigan Examiner, 3 March 1871.

Wigan Observer, 10 January 1870.